Igniting The Fire

A Woman's Guide to Setting a Blaze in ministry, business and life!

LaTracey Copeland Hughes

and

20 Igniting Women from all around the world

Igniting the Fire

Copyright © 2015

LaTracey Copeland Hughes

All rights reserved.

Igniting the Fire

DEDICATION

I'd like to dedicate this book to every co-author who decided to say "YES" to the movement! This is only the beginning and I know it hasn't been easy but it is worth it! Now, remember to put Amazon best-selling author behind your name because you earned it!
I am proud of you!

Igniting the Fire

Contents

Seasons of Change 1

The Burning Flame 11

She Said I Wouldn't, Still I Did Become 20

Healing the RAGE 30

Promiscuous to Purpose: 40

The Transformation from Cocoon to Butterfly 58

Breakdown to Breakthrough: Live Life Intentionally Courageous 70

I'm More Than You Think I Am 80

From Glowing Ashes to PRIMETIME Blaze 88

Empowered To Triumph! 98

Restored, Rebooted, Revived... Relevant Me 108

Me by Definition 118

Blessed Is She Who Believed... 128

The Struggle 130

The Process 133

FINDING LOVE FROM THE INSIDE OUT 138

The Start 139

The Struggle 142

Igniting the Fire

The Process 142

The Outcome 143

Phillis Shimamoto 146

Against All Odds…You Can Be an Overcomer! 148

Hello Sister-Friends! 148

The Start 149

The Struggle 149

The Process 153

The Outcome 156

Infidelity Didn't Win 158

My Broken Road to Destiny 168

Don't Give Up 178

IT'S TIME TO TELL THE TRUTH TO SELF 188

About the Author: 208

Igniting the Fire

Igniting the Fire

Igniting the Fire

ACKNOWLEDGMENTS

First giving honor to God in who I put my trust in! I would like to thank my husband, Preston and our four children who have stood my side throughout this journey to Igniting The Fire. This is only the beginning!
I love you all so

Igniting the Fire

Igniting the Fire

SEASONS OF CHANGE
Rosena E. Colquitt-Flynn

In order to know who I am, you must know that I am a compilation of many things and many people. I am who I am because I stand on the shoulders of Giants; many situations and people have contributed, poured into, and were weaved into the fabric of my life.

My name is Rosena E. Colquitt-Flynn; I am a child of God, the Daughter of Perry and Mary Colquitt, and sister of seven great siblings. I am the wife of almost 25 years to Greg Flynn Sr., and

Igniting the Fire

mother of Christina, Greg Jr., Brittaney and Allyssa Flynn. I am a Granddaughter, Niece, Aunt, Cousin and Friend to many.

The Start

Growing up with a large family, you aren't really prepared for the possibility of losing loved ones or friends. We tend to misbelieve that the people we love will always be around. Many struggle with death; however, I don't believe that it is death that is the real issue, but instead life after death of a loved one. The grief of knowing that the ones you once spoke to on a daily basis will no longer be there is very hard on the heart. When you're young and you lose people in your life, you know that something is wrong; you just aren't quite sure what. However, when that domino effect takes place no matter what your age is, that's when you begin to wonder what's going on. No matter how faith filled you may be, you have questions that you don't know if you'll get satisfying answers for.

Igniting the Fire

It's not always easy to be the strong one and if everyone looks to you for the strength they need, who can you turn to?

<u>The Struggle</u>

It was 2007, when we got a call that my Grandfather has passed away. Later on that year another call came in that my nephew has passed away as well. It started to seem as though it was a curse for the phone to ring. 2008 came around, and my Father took ill and, to be honest, I didn't quite know if he would make it through the year; however, he was determined to see life through to the end.

In 2009 we would experience the death that rocked us to the core… is it true? Would my Father really pass after all the heroic strength that he had shown? What was happening? Dad would give me one last hug and kiss and deliver a message of "I Love You" to be passed on to the family. Even though I knew in my heart that this would probably be the last time that I would see him and the last hug I would physically receive, I didn't want to believe it. It's

Igniting the Fire

true. Dad has also been added to the list of great ones that would pass on, and there was yet again a void and empty space in my heart, but this time my hero had received his wings, and I had to say goodbye to the first man that I ever loved. What a hard year on our family that would be, but we continued on and made it through despite our heartbreak. As the year went on, we continued to share stories of our loved ones as well as tried to comfort one another even though the sting of this one was just a bit more than we could take.

We celebrated Christmas later that year, but it just wouldn't be the same without Dad. In his honor we pressed on. The stories and memories that we shared kept us, and we just knew that God had a better plan.

As 2010 came rushing in so quickly, we ran it in and prayed that this year would be one of greatness, blessings and prosperity. Hadn't we all been through enough? At this point, things could only get better, right?

Igniting the Fire

This year I had spent a great deal of time speaking with my Aunt, praying and speaking about God's Grace and Mercy. She often let me know, that even though things would happen as they did, I should "lean not on my own understanding." Oh, how that would carry me through some tough times.

Then it happened again; August came around, and my Aunt passed on as well. Does the death of a loved one ever get any easier? I knew God had a plan that I just did not know much about, but I also knew that it just meant her job here on earth was done. It doesn't change the fact that the heart still hurts. There would be no more phone calls or letters being exchanged between us anymore. My Aunt had also received her wings. Just as I began to try and understand further what was really taking place and how transition really works, December rolled around and we received another call. This time it was my Brother who received his wings. I did my best to maintain strength, but it was just a little too much on our family. Mom is receiving this heartache from all angles; we prayed, "Lord, help us heal our broken hearts and may your will be

Igniting the Fire

done." It has been said that He never gives you more than you can take, but at this point, I just want to ask why he trusts us so much.

Once again we ring in a New Year; it is 2012, praise God. We feel a reprieve, but not for long. My health had started to take a toll on me, and just as I continued to muster up the fortitude and strength to press on in January of 2012, another call came and we were at yet another hospital. Though I was going through trials of my own, they would have to be set aside. We needed to be by Grandma's bedside, as she was taking her last breath. That's right, another angel received her wings.

This all seems so unreal, and if I had not been there myself, I would think that this could only take place in the movies. But no, this was real life. This was our life. We often thought, "How could one family experience so much pain?" Is God even listening to us anymore? I knew he had to be because we had too many good things in our lives despite our seasons of change and grief.

Igniting the Fire

We thought surely this heartache had to be over. However, we would receive another call in November 2012. My Cousin passed. He was not ill; this was unexpected.

What is going on and how do we press past this? We're not sure, we just do. The past years had been a roller coaster of emotional grief, and before we could finish grieving for one, we would find ourselves grieving for another. Still, we continue to know that God is and always will be good.

Perhaps our seasons of change and grief are over; at least we would hope so. We made it through the remainder of 2012, but not without the continued high price of heartache and pain. August of 2013, my uncle would pass, and then again a year later in August 2014, the death that takes all things over the top; another one of my Brother's would receive his wings for a death that as a family, we would find to be untimely and one of the hardest of them all.

The Process

Igniting the Fire

At some point you come to grips with all that may have taken place on life's path, and you realize that a decision must finally be made to pick up the pieces of your brokenness in order to move forward by turning your mess into your message.

I serve a very mighty God, and no matter how big my trials are, He's always there.

Seasons may change, but how you come out of it is what it makes the difference.

To all of you going through it, coming out of it, or even if you are in it–I say cheers to your seasons of change because they don't last forever and spring always follows if you can make it through your winter.

The Outcome

I have become the sum of all things, events and people in my life. While I realize that your past does not equal your future, I'm

Igniting the Fire

aware that it is because of these things, that I place such a high value on life and those whom I am blessed to have in it.

I have faced many giants and doing so has made my Faith, Love and Hope much stronger.

I may not be where I want to be, but I'm sure not where I used to be.

I'm still a work in progress, and I still walk in faith while continuing to move forward.

Diary of a Business Woman....

Rosena E. Colquitt-Flynn

Founder: Positivity Chronicle Plus LLC & Days of Positivity

positivitychronicles@yahoo.com

eye-on-u@msn.com

Igniting the Fire

Igniting the Fire

THE BURNING FLAME

Kay Matthews

I have always been the quiet type; I wouldn't say a loner, but I definitely didn't like being the center of attention. I always had the drive and mindset of an entrepreneur. So between the ages of 18 and 36, I started and maintained one successful catering and custom cake business and two non-profit organizations and became a best-selling author along the way. But the pursuit of my own happiness hasn't always been my goal. When I was finally forced by life to focus on me

Igniting the Fire

and me alone, it was then that I realized that my life was in shambles. I felt that not even God would be able to fix this big mess that had been created over time. All I know is death came knocking on my door May 29, 2013, and life has never been the same again.

The Start

I remember it like it was yesterday; I was finally free to live on my own. After living with my sister most of my life, when I turned 18 I knew that I could finally be independent. I got my own apartment; I had a job working at a small bank here in Houston, Texas. Life wasn't the greatest, but at least I had my own place and didn't have to worry about things so much. At least that's what I use to try and make myself believe. But the real truth of it all was that I was in an abusive relationship with a man I loved with all that was within me. I had never been in love before. I met him, and the way he made me feel was amazing, but hidden away from

Igniting the Fire

others was the darkness that went on behind closed doors. It was like no other. I had learned to keep quiet and hide how I felt, smile through the pain, the hurt and the emptiness that I felt only after each incident. I suffered in secret and wholeheartedly. I didn't want anyone to think I was weak. I didn't want that shameful feeling that people would or could give. So I kept quiet. There were always promises of kids of my own, but it never happened. I honestly knew that for one, that would not make our relationship better and two, why bring children into this type of environment? I was simply just at a loss, and for 7 long years I suffered not just physical abuse but mental abuse. But through it all, I knew there had to be something better out there for me. I just didn't know how I could get it.

The Struggle

I often wondered what I would do if I didn't have this man in my life. I would pray to God every night to give me better because

Igniting the Fire

I wanted better. I wanted this man I loved so much to love me without all the hate. I just wanted love that didn't come along with such harsh consequences. In the summer of 2006 after enduring so much over the years, confirmation of what I already knew was happening. By this time he had had 3 children outside the relationship, which was a constant reminder of someone telling you, "You're not good enough." I was feeling like, "God, You are truly not hearing my prayers." At that point, I decided it was time to go. I walked away with only the clothes on my back, and for 6 months I stayed with my sister until I sold our house... and so a new chapter in my life began.

But it was just the true beginning of my days and months and years in the valley, and me not realizing it. Now fast forward to the year 2013. Fully focused on my catering business and feeling truly unstoppable, I had worked so hard over the years that I had contracts coming in and, despite some hardships along the way, at this moment I was feeling very good about what was transpiring. I had been so focused the year before on getting the business in great

Igniting the Fire

standing that I had become 3rd place to everything in my life. Meaning I didn't take care of me; I was so busy planning the livelihood of my business that my health was on the line unbeknownst to me. In weeks leading up to May 29th I had been sick but just pushed through as I was always the strongest person. I didn't know any other way to be. As the days continued and I felt worse, I decided on the evening of May 28th that if I wasn't feeling better the next day, after I dropped off my clients' weeding cake I would go to the hospital. Well, I did end up in the hospital but it was not of my own volition. I was rushed to the hospital via ambulance May 29th after giving birth to a baby girl that was stillborn. My life was shattered in pieces. The most important opportunity that I often prayed for was gone. The biggest missed moment of my life I felt had been snatched away due to my own inability to notice that life was truly taking place without me. I wasn't a participant; I was just a player in the game of life, and I had just lost big.

Igniting the Fire

The Process

I was so deep in the valley at this point, I was beyond rock bottom. I felt like I was six feet under; I felt just like the walking dead. Yes, I woke up every day, and yes, I had conversations with people most of the time. But the person I was before the loss of my little girl no longer existed. I didn't want to run my business anymore. Every day was a struggle for me. I again struggled in silence. I for one didn't understand why God would do this to me. Why was he punishing me? Was I so bad of a person that I deserved this? I was mentally, physically and, most of all, spiritually broken. My life was rocked by this tragedy; I walked around with the guilt and the shame. The past abuse was nothing like this. My relationship suffered because I didn't know how to talk about how I was feeling. I could no longer speak for myself; I was no longer independent; I was truly walking alone in my own sorrow and pain. I remember going to a church picnic and sitting alone by myself with no expression on my face. Although I tried very hard to hide the way I felt, there was a lady there who would

Igniting the Fire

later become my Godmother, who walked by me and simply said, "Everything will be OK." And for the first time in all of what had happened, I believed her. She was and still is one of God's Angels here on earth. At that point, I knew that I was here for a reason. I had so many emotions day to day that I had to figure out what was normal and what wasn't. I knew that these emotions had to be more than just emotions from a lost child, so I started researching, and then it all came together. On top of the depression from the loss of my child, I was also experiencing postpartum depression. This was a subject I had never heard anyone discuss or even bring up when talking about the woes of childbirth or motherhood. I knew I wasn't alone, and that if no one was going to talk about it, I was going to start. Slowly I began to take back what was left of my life. I experienced being homeless for a short time without a car, and through it all, I stayed focused on beginning life anew because I realized through all that had happened that God kept me here for a reason.

Igniting the Fire

The Outcome

I began Babycakes and Brunch as a way to still stay connected to my passion for cooking while serving my now new purpose of helping to feed the soul though my words. I've learned so much over the years from my own experience and my past experience, but the one thing I do know for a fact is that we all truly have a purpose. God don't make no mistake in the path he has us follow and leads us down. Death came for me in the flesh May 29, 2013 at 6:43 am, but my God had the last say so. I will continue to go forth in helping women with postpartum depression because I live with it every day. I learn to maintain the emotional disconnect that comes along with it through working with others through Babycakes and Brunch. We have got to break the stigma and build a strong support system; it is the key to making my journey and those of others successful.

Kay Matthews

www.bcbtx.org

Igniting the Fire

Igniting the Fire

SHE SAID I WOULDN'T, STILL I DID BECOME.....
Ophelia Nixon Uke

As a child there were so many things I remember being told I would never be. I always knew that in our household there were favorites amongst us, and I was not nor would I ever be seen as one. The memories of the hurts sometimes try to give access for the bitterness to resurface, but what good would that is for me and the person I've become? Plus, why hold on to what I've worked so long and hard to release? Instead of dwelling on what was, I'm filled with gratitude and love for God as He found favor in me. I was filled

Igniting the Fire

with strength to redesign the life of a little girl that almost wasn't, because the person I desired to hear the words of motivation, love and inspiration from never came through. I was torn down with diabolical words of worthlessness which were spoken over my life.

It was during those moments my desire for life slipped away as I had already forgone my dreams of one day being someone of worth. As I'm sharing my journey, I can smile at every line written and the spoken words of lies told to me about all things I wouldn't be, and smile a well about all that I did become. Here's the thing I came to fully understand--when God has a calling upon your life, no matter what man says or does, it cannot alter what God is going to do with you and for you.

The Start

Vague are my memories when everything in life seemed as perfect and happy as we would want them to be. Nonetheless, if I'm to push my mind hard enough to reflect back on such moments

Igniting the Fire

no matter how far and in between they might be, there is a few which I truly wish would have lingered. As a child in Jamaica, I could remember playing in the yard with my eldest brother and my cousin, as we did all the things we were asked repetitively not to do by my grandmother.

Without fail, daily we could be found climbing the trees, jumping the fence or running around throwing stones as the sound of our laughter would enter to fill every corner of my grandmother's house. This place that I was blessed to call home before leaving the soils of Jamaica possessed a strong family dynamic wherein the presence of God could always be felt. All who entered in knew the rules of the home; though my grandmother was stern, she embraced all with love.

It was the kind of home that whether you were family, friend or foe, her behavior towards each person wasn't altered. However, how one chose to interpret it, was solely left up to him or her. It was my place of comfort and happiness with a wonderful

Igniting the Fire

beginning; unfortunately, plans were made which gave me over to a life I would soon regret.

The Struggle

I have now entered into a foreign world which bore no resemblance to the place where I was born, the place I knew to be home... my home. Everything was so different; I understood nothing, for even the house which was to become my place of residence was completely different from the one I had known and loved.

This place that I prayed would bring me joy because it consisted of my parents and siblings quickly turned into the place that introduced me to a world of self-loathing and bitterness, which none should ever come to know. My life no longer allowed me to smile on a continuous basis, for just as quickly as it was loaned to me, it seemed to be confiscated even faster causing me to evolve into a withdrawn child.

Igniting the Fire

With time my heart developed a love-hate relationship towards many things in life, including the people I was surrounded by. How was I to love unconditionally when my name was taken from me repetitively and replaced by terms that were neither nice nor endearing?

The older I got, the more the pain of living increased as it daily held my hand when all I truly yearned for was it to let me go. I cried and prayed that life could hate me just as much as I had grown to hate it, for if it could hate me with the same intensity then maybe, just maybe, we could say our final goodbyes. The blueprints my mother designed for my life placed me on a street corner per her words, because not only was I ugly and worthless, but I was so unlovable that no one would ever want me, as my usage was for one purpose only.

What had she wished upon my life, why was this her wish for me? I was a mere child searching to know who I was, while she busied herself to destroy any positive dreams, hopes and aspirations of possibilities life had to offer. Each time my eyes closed, her words

Igniting the Fire

were like a record which was permanently set on replay. I sought for ways to silence the noise her words created in my head; the more I fought them, the stronger they became. When those negative seeds were planted and fed, all self-worth became lost, as the distortions deeply rooted themselves so that my reflection and I were now strangers to each other.

The person I saw on a regular basis was extremely ugly; my existence was a waste. My heart began to solidify due to the fact that the foundation of the home was built upon mental, physical and emotional abuse which caused disruption to my internal garden that was being invaded by weeds of hatred. Funny enough, though the atmosphere of the home was not a loving one, it provided us stability.

Honestly, I would have relinquished stability for love. We were brought up in church and taught to pray; therefore, I knew God and who He was. Still, I was left wondering where he was and if he was near, and if so, why did it feel as if He had forsaken me.

Igniting the Fire

Feeling lost to myself and abandoned by God, I knew I still could not fully release my grasp on Him though it did loosen.

The Process

The more I gave up pieces of me, the more hurts were stacked upon my back. I soon became incapable of thinking people could ever be honest with me, even when they tried to persuade me of the goodness I possessed and the amazing things that I would one day do. To me those words were laughable; I was convinced they didn't know what they were saying.

I remembered times when I would outright look some of these very people in the face telling them they needed to stop lying. I was so broken that not even the beauty which was my reflection could be seen. Everything my mother said I believed because why would she lie? That was my mother, she was unable to lie about the person I was; therefore, all things she said had to be true.

Once I stopped listening to her words and started focusing more on God, things became more tolerable as life became more livable.

Igniting the Fire

I needed to face my demons of self-hate and insecurities which plagued me relentlessly, for no matter what I thought or tried death refused me. God gave me a gift, one of which forced me to change my mindset for if not her fate would have mimicked that which was said to be mine.

This precious gift was my daughter, she became the mirror that I had to view myself through in order to be the woman God designed me to be, but more-so the mother my children needed and the wife my husband deserved.

The Outcome

My journey wasn't an easy one, but it was extremely rewarding. Sometimes we sit back reminiscing over the struggles we've faced, wondering how we overcame so much, especially when life seemed so dim as hope was lost. My willingness to fight as I was now determined to survive for my family, the family God gave to me, made everything worthwhile. Today I stand in a place of confidence that was once overshadowed by a heavy cloud of

Igniting the Fire

darkness, which did not provide a way for the light of a new day to set in. This future that I was told I couldn't have become the mapping of an even greater path which I never dreamt possible, especially for me, a path which I could look at with love, respect and admiration.

Too many times we have given more ear than what is truly deserved to the entertaining of negativity; it's time for us to take a good look at ourselves and believe in whom God created us to be. No longer do I rely on the perception of man; I validate me for I know who I am. I am... the Soul Empowerer! #SoulEmpowerer #TIGERCONFIDENCE

Ophelia Uke

www.opheliauke.com

Igniting the Fire

HEALING THE RAGE
Yuoranda Walker

I am a survivor, and sharing my truth gives me the opportunity to help other women realize that they can be survivors too. My truth is one that I used to be ashamed of. One that I believed allowed me to be mean, hateful, scared, and even detrimental to my own wellbeing. My truth is most likely one you have heard before…maybe from a family member or a close friend. It could even be a truth that you carry with you day in and day out of your everyday life.

My truth could be the one deep dark secret that you have been scared to share with others for fear of judgment. I understand

Igniting the Fire

because my truth held me captive for many years and put me in a deep dark place at one point in my life. It had me in a place that I still shutter at from time to time when I think about it. A place that I'd much rather forget about, but I know that I am unable to simply because it is MY TRUTH and it must be shared. It must be shared not for sympathy or revenge but solely for the glory of God.

By now you may be asking, "What is this truth?" Well, before I get to that let me share this: When we refuse to acknowledge that we need healing, we destroy ourselves. When we refuse to do the work to obtain that healing, we destroy our future generations.

I did not want any part in destroying my future generations, so I had to take a stand and break the chains that had me bound. The chains of child sexual abuse, rape, rage, & self-hate.

The Start

My mother and father divorced when I was too young to remember. My mother later remarried my stepfather, and he became my example of a father, husband, & a man. His example

Igniting the Fire

was a poor one but the only one I had and since I had no choice in the matter, he became the one I looked at every day.

It was from his example that I grew up knowing what type of man not to get involved with, but it also made me into the mother, wife, and woman that I didn't want to become. My stepfather was once the point of origin for my hate…my hate for life and the hate I held towards myself. As a young girl, he became my predator instead of my protector. I was not only his stepdaughter, but also his stepped-on abuse victim. From a very young age until my junior year in high school, the man I called dad sexually abused me.

He took his own insecurities, self-hate, and abusive mentality and transferred them to me. He gave me his pains because he was not taught how to deal with them the proper way. His idea of dealing with his hurt and pain was to put it on someone else. I was just one of the people who were on the receiving end of what he had to offer. My mother and my two brothers also received his mess--my mother by way of extreme physical and harsh mental abuse and my brothers by way of mental abuse and poor leadership.

Igniting the Fire

Although I told my mother about the abuse at age ten, she was too lost herself to understand the importance of protecting me. I needed her to be my strength, but instead she fell into her own weaknesses and chose to believe the lies her husband told her. And so my hell continued many years thereafter, leading to me being placed in the Georgia Foster Care System at 16 and aging out of that same system at the age of 17.

The Struggle

It was because of the sexual and mental abuse by my stepfather, the constant fighting between him and my mother, seeing my mother drink herself into a stupor more times than I care to remember—because of these things I grew into a young girl who hated the world, hated herself and was full of rage.

I became a shell of a person, just living life day to day while putting on a fake smile and trying to please everyone. Because I didn't have the tools to overcome the pain and hurt from my horror

Igniting the Fire

story, I became mean, hateful, and hopeless (in my eyes). I remember just wanting to die and even attempting suicide twice.

My first attempt was after being raped in the ninth grade by a so-called boyfriend. I didn't attempt the suicide because I was raped; I attempted the suicide because when my mother found out about the rape, she turned on me and made me feel as though I was a dirty whore. She made me feel unloved and unwanted, and so I believed death was the only way that all the pain and hurt I carried would go away.

The second attempt was during my second marriage. This was a marriage built on a junior high school love that I believed in my heart would last till the end of time. I was in my early 20's with two small children and still hurting from all that I had endured as a child. I was also hurting because my husband did not find me attractive due to weight gain from having children, which drove me to fits of jealousy and fighting.

Igniting the Fire

I remember sitting at a red light in a daze wishing I was dead and just taking my foot off the brake and slowly rolling into traffic. I was confident that death was the only way to stop the deep inner pain. I actually believed that my children, whom I loved, would be better off without me. I knew by taking my foot off the brake, cars and trucks would slam into my car and I would die instantly. But God had a different plan for my life because as I began to roll, the light turned green and I was shaken out of my daze by the car behind me blowing its horn.

At that moment all I could do was cry because God's plan for my life was not my plan for my life. He apparently saw bigger and better for me. That day He showed me that He was directing this story, not me.

The Process

It was many years after my second suicide attempt that I received a breakthrough of sorts. I separated from my second husband and moved to a new state. By this time I had three

Igniting the Fire

children and needed a new start. Houston, TX became our new home. I knew I did not have the support of many, but I didn't care. I needed this for me. I had to prove to myself that I could make it. I knew it would not be easy, and it wasn't.

I experienced another rape while my children were asleep in their beds; I experienced living in a home with mice and being terrified to go to sleep; I experienced walking miles in the early morning before the sun came up and miles in the burning heat with my two youngest children; I experienced begging strangers for money to feed my children, and I experienced being homeless at a homeless shelter. Now I know all of that doesn't sound like much of a breakthrough to you, but in essence, it was that and more. I had to go through all of those things to get to my true breaking point, the point where I made the decision to stop living my life for me and to start living it for God. While sitting at the homeless shelter, God showed me how through everything I endured, HE still protected me, and I realized that all that I had been through was for a reason.

Igniting the Fire

The Outcome

Allowing myself to submit to God's divine will that night at the homeless shelter saved my life and the lives of my children. Since then I have flourished greatly and have learned to not only forgive the ones who hurt me, but also to forgive myself. I learned the importance of healing my hurt and loving myself. Who and what I was years ago…victim, cutter, depressed, hurt, defeated, alone, and lost is far from who I am today…SURVIVOR, HEALED, SECURE, IN PEACE & HAPPY. Today I am a self-published author, founder of my own organization, advocate for child sexual abuse & rape, a loving mother & wife but, most importantly, I am a servant of God and a survivor willing to share my story to help others. I am not ashamed to tell my truth because it always ends the same, with God getting the praise & glory that HE so deserves. I believe everything happens for a reason. I endured what I did so that I could help others heal their hurt while giving glory to our Almighty Lord and Savior!

Yuoranda Walker

Igniting the Fire

Igniting the Fire

Promiscuous to Purpose:
Faith, Forgiveness, Fortitude & Favor

Shelita Winfield

When **they** came to a place called Skull, there they crucified him, along with the criminals—one on his right, the other one on his left, Jesus said "Father, forgive them, for they do not know what they are doing." Luke 23:33-34

Lord knows, I didn't know what I was doing all those years. Here is my journey:

The Start

Igniting the Fire

My story is not the typical story of tragedy to triumph or victim to victory that so many people have experienced. However, I was a victim to my own self-inflicted abuse and self-sabotaging behaviors that I exhibited and decisions I made throughout the years.

I was raised in a two-parent household until the age of 13 when my parents decided this would be their final split. I (more so than my brother who was 6 years old at the time) had seen this happen before. My parents would argue, fuss and fight. My dad would leave and at some point he'd come back. I don't recall there being any physical abuse, but there was plenty of yelling and cussing. But when times were good, they were good. My parents had friends and parties and music and liquor and pokeno!!! And it was fun. It was fun to sit at the top of the steps, listening to the grown folks' conversation. Sometimes I could hang around until bedtime, sometimes a little later. I just remember that when it was good…it was good!!!

Igniting the Fire

And then there were my grandparents. My maternal grandmother, Dottie, is a short, feisty thing. Completely outspoken, very opinionated, no real tact but funny as all get out!!! My cousin, brother and I would go over there, and she was always in the kitchen cooking, cigarette hanging out of her mouth and a beer (in a glass) on the table. She used to drink those little green cans of Rolling Rock, and my cousin and I used to sneak sips from those little cans. My cousin was always in trouble for something or another. Dottie would always be fussing at him to get a switch from the tree so she could tear his behind up. I am the only girl so I never got in trouble.

My parental grandparents, well, were "different." There was no Rolling Rock, but there were dry martinis and a brown liquor. Every house had some form of alcohol, and every house had an abundance of love. My paternal grandmother, Grandma Lil, loved to shop, and she loved to travel. I picked up both those traits from her. But more than that, she loved the Lord. I went to church most Sundays with her. Rev Nichols would preach, and I'd fall asleep

Igniting the Fire

on the warmth and softness of my grand mom's black mink coat. At church there was candy and there were boys...and I liked them both.

So, I'm 13 years old, my parents have split up, my mom is hurting, my dad is single, and I'm hitting puberty. While I began having the time of my life (so I thought), the enemy began to plant seeds of self-condemnation, self-hate and a blaming mindset, and I looked to boys for the love I thought was gone. I don't quite know what I blamed myself for but I do know that boys were everywhere.

So my parents are divorcing, and I lost my virginity. Yep, at 13. And then I get pregnant. My parents are fighting, I'm pregnant, and it only makes sense for me to get an abortion.

My parents are divorcing, I've lost my virginity, and I've had my first abortion. My parents are still fighting, I'm still a teenager, and I keep getting pregnant again and again and again. Abortion, abortion after abortion.

Igniting the Fire

Pain after pain after pain. Boy after boy after boy. Pain on top of pain on top of pain.

So, I'm 17, and everyone wants me to go to college, except me. School was never a problem but boys were. Ironically, I went to an all girls' high school but despite that, boys were everywhere. At the urging of family and some teachers, I went off to college. And the world opened up. There were boys and men. Parties and alcohol. Freedom and accessibility. And there were no parents, no rules, and no guidelines.

So, I did what I'd always done. I had sex. And I got pregnant. And I had an abortion. I think there were seven in total. So life and men continued. They'd come, they'd go, and some would even come back around. It felt like a revolving door leading into and out of an empty space. I had always known of God, but I had not known God for myself. What I remember most during this time is the sense of feeling empty, the sense of wondering why I couldn't pick right, why I couldn't have that love from one man. Why I wasn't good enough to say yes to? So they continued to come and

Igniting the Fire

go. Come and go. Some came back around but none of them stayed.

The Struggle:

I had gone on to become fairly accomplished in my career throughout all of this. For the most part, my life was good until it came to men. And my choices in men almost cost me everything.

I met a man who told a story, a story of music and money and a great life style. I bought his story hook, line and sinker. He'd come down from New York and stay with me. I never thought it odd that he took Greyhound every time he came down. He'd come down, and we had fun. I felt totally special, totally like the only one. We went out, we talked and shared dreams, and it felt like a relationship.

On this particular trip he came down with some friends (male and female). I never saw the woman, but the other friend did come past the house. The NBA finals were on, and I was in the kitchen frying

Igniting the Fire

chicken wings. Next thing I know, I see a blast of light, and I'm looking down the nozzle of a nine millimeter gun. The drug police were in my house, and a raid was in progress. I'm handcuffed and I'm crying and hyperventilating. And the police are tearing up my small apartment. As quick as the light flashed, the guy was gone, and I was there all alone with the police. It was only by the grace of God that nothing was at my house. The detective sat me down and proceeded to tell me the truth. They'd been watching him for quite some time, every visit, every call, and every move. And they had been checking me out as well. He figured I knew nothing and had no involvement. He knew about my job and my commute to work and my comings and goings. You see, he had secured a state driver's license with my address on it. And voile…I was on the radar.

But God is faithful, and He had a ram in the bush for me. You see, my job involved going back and forth to court for my clients, so I got to know some of the judges. One of the judges who, of course, was an attorney was able to secure an attorney for me. I

Igniting the Fire

had to go to the courts and wait to see if they were going to indict me. There was no indictment... Thank God, and I was able to walk away and continue on with my life. I heard he ended up doing time, but to this day I have no idea. God allowed me to walk away from that, and I never turned back!!!

But I had to start over, and my trust factor of everyone, especially myself was shot!!!

In the midst of this I met a young woman at training. We became fast friends and despite the partying her family introduced me back to church. They accepted me as is and showed Godly love towards me. That taught me that God also loved me as is. Her family made it acceptable again to go to church. It was ok for me to go to church, and that's what I started doing. Her brother and I dated off and on for years, but it was never too serious. At some point we stopped seeing each other, and I met someone and returned to Philly. Well...that didn't work at all, and I went back down south. But a transition began. I remember very distinctly saying... well, crying out to God that I realized that no man could

Igniting the Fire

ever fill the void, that empty black hole that I've been experiencing all this time. Only God could fill that space. And so the transition began.

I returned back to Virginia, and I began to go to church regularly and actively. My old friend and I reconnected and picked up right where we left off…on and off. No real commitment. No real expectations.

And then I met a man. A man that brought interest and excitement and passion and challenge and everything that I wanted and looked for. I could've loved him except that he lived with his girlfriend. But we had our times…over and over and over. And it was good. And it was passionate. And it was intense. And it got me pregnant. Again . But this was different. I was different. And I decided to have this child. And that's when he told me she was pregnant as well.

So, here I am…alone and pregnant. And then there were complications. But in the midst of this…I met another man, a

Igniting the Fire

superman. He knew I was pregnant, and he didn't care. He wanted to get to know me. Spend time with me. Care for me and take care of me. So when I was hospitalized for 5 weeks with pregnancy complications, my Superman was right there. Here is where I must say that if you don't slow down and heed the Word of God, He will slow you down.

For five weeks I was in the hospital. Superman was there so often and so long the hospital staff presumed he was the father. And he never disputed that. After three false delivery episodes (I'm not even at 6 months yet), I give birth to my son by cesarean. My son is severely premature, extremely underdeveloped, just a little more than a pound, and he dies 1 week after he was born. There were no words then nor are there any words now to describe or explain what that feels like. But the guilt was immeasurable. After all the babies I aborted, the child I longed to have and keep was the one to serve as the sacrifice for all my poor choices. And that guilt I carried for all those years for all those abortions came rushing upon me. It was then that I realized I had been living in guilt and

Igniting the Fire

shame for well over 20 years. And I had to accept that the death of my son was the culmination of all the death I created.

The Process

Eventually I relocated north of where I was but was going back and forth to Richmond for church. On this one particular evening during a woman's event, there was an alter call for women who had had an abortion(s). I found myself at the altar, being prayed for and bam…slain in the Spirit. But I was different and recognized I had a lot of work to do. So I went back home, joined the church and allowed the Holy Spirit and my Pastor to truly minister to my spirit. And I served. And I did my work. And I got married. And I got divorced. And I continued to do my work, and I continued to serve, and I continued to be ministered to.

And I began to become honest and transparent with myself. I allowed myself to acknowledge that I was angry at myself for all those choices. And the men. And the pregnancies. And the

Igniting the Fire

abortions. And the decisions. And the ignored flags. And the mistakes. And the disappointments. And the lost friends. And the missed opportunities. And the…everything.

And then I got sick…really sick. But God is a keeper. And he kept me. He kept me through it all. And even through illness, not only did I get physically and spiritually stronger, I got emotionally stronger.

The key to that was learning how to forgive myself, letting go of all the hurt and pain that I was holding on to that I inflicted onto myself.

What to do when you need to forgive you?

Forgiving yourself is probably one of the hardest things a person has to do. Why? For starters, because you have to be open, honest and transparent with you!! You have to recognize and acknowledge the choices, decisions and reasons that bring you to the place you are in and then accept that there is no one to change you and your situation but you. Even though we are our own worst

Igniting the Fire

critic, it's tough accepting that you ultimately placed yourself in this place of unforgiveness...this place of bitterness...this place of not loving self.

When you think forgiving yourself is necessary and when you think you are ready to forgive yourself, think about how you have forgiven others and think about releasing yourself from the pain just like you released them. The person you are is comprised of a myriad of situations, experiences, perceptions and decisions. Sometimes well, you just don't get it right, and you must give yourself room to make mistakes. "Forgive yourself for your faults and mistakes and move on." Les Brown.

The bible says, "In this world you will have trouble. But take heart! I have overcome the world." Your past mistakes have helped shape the person that you are today. Don't look at them as mistakes, but look at them as the steps along the journey.

Igniting the Fire

Self-forgiveness is a journey. Not a destination. There is no timetable and no right or wrong way to flow through the process. Ultimately, accepting who you, love yourself, making decisions that will improve your situation and learning from the setbacks that will ultimately come is what will ignite and sustain the fire that burns inside each one of us.

Your mistakes do not define you, but your decisions will dictate the path to your destiny.

The Outcome

Despite all the disappointments, I learned that no person, place or thing could fill the void that had been there for so long. I learned to hear the voice of God and accepted and embraced the fact that only He could fill that black abyss that was consuming me. So I got back to God and His Word and began to flourish again. But life happened, and after the death of my infant son, a cheating spouse and subsequent divorce from my presumed "best friend," I realized

Igniting the Fire

that I needed to take a hard fast look at myself and my decisions. It was during this process that I learned there really is a "blessing in the brokenness" and that I couldn't grow past my pains. I began to examine the root of my choices--promiscuity, entitlement, multiple abortions and men, and realized that I was operating in unforgiveness which had turned into bitterness, and that bitterness was toward my very own self.

God began to minister to me in Word and deed, and I reached a place of self-forgiveness and then forgiveness of all those I blamed along the way.

The result is a Godly woman who can stand before God's people and know what it means to hate yourself but through God's love and grace come to a place of self-love, respect, admiration and wholeness.

UNLIMITED WINNING PRINCIPLES:

1. Have a relationship with God. Pray, attend a bible teaching church, tithe 10%, give of time, talent and treasure, be active

Igniting the Fire

and SERVE!!!

2. Pursue your purpose and destiny. We are all here and created to give God glory. Ask Him what He wants you to do, and give God all the glory in doing it.

3. Be honest and transparent with those you are in relationship with. People may not like what you say, but they will respect you for saying it.

4. Be honest and transparent with yourself. Kidding yourself is useless because you'll be unhappy with the results. Then have the audacity to wonder why.

5. Identify your "BE YOU" Team. Have a small group of people for the common sense test, the accountability test, the honesty test, the spiritual test and the exhortation test. You pour out to others but who is supporting, celebrating, praying and cheering you on?

6. Don't be afraid to network. People won't get to know how fabulous you are if you stay home or travel in the same circles.

Igniting the Fire

7. Invest in yourself…financially, educationally, spiritually and emotionally.

8. Do what you love…whether it's working for yourself or working for someone else, do what you are passionate about. If you're doing #1, God will take care of the resources.

9. Always look great…keep your hair done; wear properly fitting clothes and sharp comfortable shoes. You never know where you'll end up or who you will be in the presence of. Always be ready to accept an invitation because there may be an opportunity awaiting you.

10. Talk to everyone!!! Don't be afraid to speak to strangers (just don't run off with them). Be comfortable talking, networking and sharing the gift you are and the gifts you have with those that God directs you to. Be a SERVANT.

Today, well today I am the BOSS (Business Owners Strategic Success) Coach, helping women entrepreneurs achieve unlimited wins in life, business and ministry. As a life coach, I am igniting

Igniting the Fire

the world with my BOSS roadmap where we focus on the inner game (values/beliefs) and the outer champion (leadership and success). This culminates in a confident woman who is secure in herself and is equipped to gift her tribe with all that God has purposed for her to do.

SheWin Unlimited... because of God's unlimited love, I truly am living an unlimited life.

Shelita Winfield

www.shewinunlimited.com

shelita@shewinunlimited.com

Igniting the Fire

THE TRANSFORMATION FROM COCOON TO BUTTERFLY
Danielle Reece

Life's journey has many ups and downs. My journey began at the age of 4. My earliest childhood memory was one of intense pain and confusion. Although it was my earliest, it wouldn't be my only memory of sexual abuse. The abuse in conjunction with early exposure to pornography set me on a pathway of destruction. It wasn't until later that the Holy Spirit revealed to me just how much of an impact those situations had on my life.

Igniting the Fire

The Start

My mother and father divorced when I was 7 years old. This left me feeling abandoned and further reinforced my mistrust. What small amount of security I had was stripped from me. My father moved on, remarried, and had another child. I felt as if I were no longer a priority in his life. Visits were hit and miss, and our relationship changed tremendously after the divorce. Like many women today, I too had "Daddy issues."

The Struggle

My greatest obstacles were mistrust and lust. I was molested by a close family member whom I trusted. The breach of that trust caused me to not trust anyone. For years, I never trusted anyone, and I lived in constant fear of being betrayed or hurt by those close to me. So I began to build a wall to guard myself from being hurt

Igniting the Fire

or victimized anymore. I began to develop a personality that was not who God destined for me to be. I learned, after a while, that the very wall I was using to keep away the bad, was also keeping away the good. Remember, a callused heart can't feel pain or love.

The other obstacle I encountered was lust. Being exposed to sexual activity at such a young age is very traumatic. I spent many years confused about my sexuality. I felt ashamed and dirty for the things I had experienced and for the things I had seen.

I realize now, the traumatic situations I experienced were tactics of the enemy to reroute my course of life. Those situations were seeds planted in my mind and soul that began to grow over time. They created a root system that was the origin of my thoughts and actions for years to come.

This unhealthy view of sex led me to lose my virginity and become pregnant at the age of 17. Fear, immaturity, and other influences led to a hasty decision to have an abortion. This decision led to

Igniting the Fire

even more feelings of guilt and unworthiness. At such a young age, I felt the weight of the world on my shoulders.

I felt as if I had already experienced so much, and somehow I blamed myself for it all. Mentally, I understood the episodes of victimization were not my fault. However, subconsciously I still blamed myself.

My actions proved that I was angry at the world and myself. Subsequently, I began to use alcohol and marijuana to mask the pain I felt inside. I knew it didn't solve my problems, but it took my mind off of them for the time being.

A few years later my high school sweetheart proposed, I said yes, and shortly thereafter I moved out of my mother's house and into an apartment with him. Aside from my short time in college, this was my first real taste of freedom and, boy, did I indulge.

We threw many parties that consisted of alcohol consumption and heavy marijuana usage. A few months later, we got married but

Igniting the Fire

still continued our lifestyle. It wasn't until I became pregnant with my first child that I decided to clean my life up.

I figured if I had to stop smoking for nine months, I might as well just quit all together. So I did. I cleaned up my life, got back into church, and enrolled back in school. I refused to bring a child into this world under those circumstances. I wanted to live my life in a way my daughter could be proud of. A few years passed, and I became pregnant with my second child. I continued to better myself for the sake of my family. However, my husband continued to live the lifestyle we lived prior to starting a family. His drinking and smoking increased to the point he became verbally and emotionally abusive.

For years I remained in that relationship, praying and believing God for a change. Unfortunately, it wasn't my husband's desire to change, and God will never force us or go against our will. Once I realized our marriage was coming to an end, I too began to drink heavily.

Igniting the Fire

Although I was ready to part ways, it was still very painful to end a five-year marriage and a twelve-year friendship. So I resorted to my old habits of bringing, what I thought at the time was, comfort.

Fast forwarding about four years, I remarried and had 2 more children. Life was fairly decent. I was working as a Licensed Practical Nurse for five years, and God began to impress on my heart to quit working. I struggled with this idea for many months. I can admit now that I was operating in unbelief. First, I felt as if I had worked too hard for my nursing degree and license to just stop working.

Then, I didn't believe that my family would be as financially secure as we were at the time. Nonetheless, I eventually submitted and I became a stay-at-home mom. Although I enjoyed having more time with my children, after a couple of years I became depressed and bored. I began to sink into the too familiar rut I had visited many times in life.

Igniting the Fire

I thought, "Is there not more to life than this?" Literally, all I did was take the kids to school, clean, cook, and run errands. This is where I found my "rock bottom." When I say "rock bottom," I don't just mean hard times. I mean, literally feeling like you are at your wits end; like if God didn't show up soon, I would lose my mind. I felt restless in my spirit, and I could not shake it. So I began to search. I prayed, I searched the word, and searched within myself.

The more I prayed for direction, the more God would reveal to me. The work began with me. I realized that my life could not change until I did. I had to face my demons head on. This required me being honest and transparent with myself. It also required an intense level of forgiveness for myself and others. I had to do the work necessary for a life transformation.

You can't wait on someone to ignite your fire; you have to do it. I believe when we take one step forward, God takes three steps. Pull those goals and dreams off the shelf, and blow the dust off of them. Activate it with your faith.

Igniting the Fire

The Process

During this phase, I also had to deal with unworthiness. It didn't matter how many accomplishments I had or how well I looked to people on the outside, I still felt unworthy. So when I was awakened by the Holy Spirit one morning and told to create business cards, you can imagine the level of confusion I dealt with. Why me, God? I didn't even know where or how to create a business card, let alone run a business. I felt so inadequate for the assignment I was given.

I have sat in meetings with CEOs and business owners and didn't have a clue as to what they were talking about. I literally had to fake it until I made it. I obeyed the call. I silenced the voice of my enemy and my inner me.

Igniting the Fire

Step by step, the Holy Spirit led and directed me where to go. He has connected me with everyone and everything I have needed for this journey.

He has even used my business to open the door for me to speak into the lives of others. So when he instructed me to write my first book, "The Overcomer," I quickly obliged because I now have a revelation that it is His work. He orchestrates and makes provision for His work. I am simply the vessel he has chosen to bring it forth.

The Outcome

I am certainly not where I desire to be, but I can unequivocally say that I have grown tremendously. As I look back on the many obstacles the enemy put in my path to make me stumble and abort God's purpose within me, I'm amazed. Many couldn't and many didn't make it, but I did. I am far from perfect. However, I have so much peace now.

Igniting the Fire

Peace in knowing that He who has begun a good work in me is faithful to complete it. So now I sit back, like the rest of the world, and watch the story unfold. God has birthed things out of me that I never knew existed. He has strengthened and anointed me for tasks I never imagined I could accomplish. So now I understand. I no longer feel any resentment, self-pity, or guilt over my past. It ALL worked together for my good.

I believe we are all born with a fire. God deposits within us everything we need to carry out our destiny. However, at the very moment of our birth, the enemy begins his plot to snuff out our fire. Pain, disappointment, and crises are like water; with every drop our fire begins to fizzle out. It is our job to re-ignite the fire within us. The Holy Spirit is our oxygen.

A fire cannot burn without oxygen. Neither can we thrive without Him. Lastly, our faith is the wood. It takes wood to keep the fire going. Despite all odds, we must keep applying our faith to our life, our situations, and our purposes so that our fire can remain ignited.

Danielle Reece (www.DanielleReece.org)

Igniting the Fire

Igniting the Fire

BREAKDOWN TO BREAKTHROUGH: LIVE LIFE INTENTIONALLY COURAGEOUS

Dr. Carolyn Treadwell-Butler PhD, CLC

I have sinned; what shall I do unto thee, O thou preserver of men: why hast though set me as a mark against thee, so that I am a burden to myself?
Job 7:20

Breakdowns---Everyone has them. They are those moments when who you are or have become is no longer effective in successfully meeting the

Igniting the Fire

expectations in life. Breakdowns are those points in life where you are suffering mentally, emotionally, socially and physically. They are those points in life where beliefs, values and assumptions are challenged. You are operating from habits, routines, and rituals which don't require much thought; you are just going through the motions. Externally, you are a picture of strength and courage to others. Internally, you are broken.

What I have learned in my life is that bad things happen to good people. For most of my life I felt that I was a burden not only to my life but to everyone else. Through it all, God has been my comforter and source of strength. This chapter is about me living my life intentionally courageous. I had to learn to love me as God loved me despite the events that occurred in my life that caused me to feel worthless.

The Start

Igniting the Fire

The perfect life for a Christian woman when I was growing up was to get married and have children. I had graduated from high school and attended some college, but I had aspirations to be a wife and mother. During the early eighties my two daughters were born, and they were the center of my world. As a mother, I wanted the best for them. We were a one-income family, and our finances were just enough to take care of our basic needs. It was a happy time for me.

I was fortunate enough to be able to stay at home with my children until they started school. As they got older, there were additional expenses, so I had to find a job. Once I started working, I really enjoyed it. During that time the Bill Cosby show was a favorite pastime for me. The Huxtables motivated me enough to go back to school and pursue a career. The end result was that I did graduate from college and I had a lucrative paying job. We were able to afford to purchase a home, cars and keep money in the bank.

Igniting the Fire

By the time my children were grown, I was in a second marriage and completing graduate school. The only thing that was missing from my life at that time was a relationship with God. I had been raised in the church and baptized at a young age. I knew my calling was to teach, and at nine years old I would seek out people to talk about God with. Life happens, as they say, and I got off course. It took prayer and studying God's word to get me back to where I first believed. It was a great witnessing time for me as well; I witnessed my husband and stepson give their life to Christ. Another milestone in life started when I was accepted into a doctoral program, and I began teaching in the university. Our blended family was also growing with the birth of our grandchildren. We were financially able to purchase a larger home and take vacations as often as we wanted. Our next milestone was to be planning for our retirement. Then something happened that disrupted that flow. The world around me just didn't make sense anymore.

Igniting the Fire

The Struggle

My mother died. I didn't realize how much of an anchor she was in my life. My mother's death really took its toll on me. I was completely knocked off guard by it. Life became a series of routines, along with problems and disappointments; you accept your lot in life and keep pushing. I was living life as I had learned it; I was programmed with thoughts of accepting mediocrity. Unconsciously, I was constantly fighting this voice inside that declared that I was not good enough and I didn't deserve it. Despite all that I had been able to accomplish, at the end of the day I was not having the breakthroughs that I imagined.

The morning that I woke up and realized that I did not know the person looking back at me in the mirror was the scariest time in my life. A series of life events left me in a world where I was no longer a wife, a daughter or a mother; that is not as it had been scripted for me the last 50 years. I was still healing from a heart attack and surgery when my husband decided he wanted to be with

Igniting the Fire

someone other than me. Every material thing that I had worked hard to get was taken from me.

In the moment of the breakdown, the knowledge of oneself, perception of the world and reality all collide. I was limited; thus it seemed that suffering and discomfort were all that was left. The boundaries that were invisible now were quite apparent. Each traumatic event leads to dying moments---a little of whom you know yourself to be dies each time. Our minds serve us just what we are ordering during these breakdowns--sorrow, pain and self-pity. In my lifetime I have had many of these dying moments--divorce, loss of children, sexual abuse, job loss, and all my worldly possessions gone. My mother had posed a question to me some years back: Are you living or just existing? I knew the answer to the question and I answered it---I am just existing. There were many days the pain was so great, and I did not understand why God was allowing me to hurt so bad. I recalled Job's affliction and how he had been through so much that he longed for death. I understood.

Igniting the Fire

For several years after that moment, I was left in of place of darkness and despair. In my own secret place I realized I had been fighting depression, loneliness and self-doubt for years. Breakdowns can show up as thought loops that go around and around in the mind—of course, leading nowhere. As I have done so many times and for so long, I placed everything in the back of my mind and moved on. I filled my life with doing stuff and staying busy so that I did not have to feel the pain. I got to this point in my life where I prayed to God and I asked him to just let me see myself as he sees me. I was so tired of pretending to be this strong and happy person.

The Process

God granted me my request to see myself as he sees me. I was in the mirror one morning when I saw myself for the very first time. It was then I realized that I was still living my life as a victim of sexual abuse. Every decision that I made was because I never

Igniting the Fire

loved myself; love was a feeling taken from me years ago. It takes living intentionally courageous to go from breakdown to breakthrough. The change has to be about you and for you. What does an intentional courageous life look like? It is a life that is deliberately designed by you. It means approaching life responsibly and purposely, with goals in mind of which you are and about what you want out of life. It is about living consciously, being awake with intentions versus wandering and operating on biases, experiences, and expectations of others. An intentional life is one with a definite direction. It is about not accepting what we have been accepting from others as our truth without intentionally deciding that we agree. We have a specific God-given calling and purpose. We have a God-given mission. We have to be in pursuit of our mission. We must define the specific mission in our own lives. Awakening to a new life and new meaning to life is yet another journey to begin. Everything you want to achieve in life is dependent upon you being you.

Igniting the Fire

The Outcome

There have been some definite changes in my lifestyle, some prioritizing, some behavioral changes, some belief changes and commitment changes. I decide what is successful in my life, not anyone else. I do not have to play the roles that have been given to me. I am living the life that God has planned for me. (Jeremiah 29:11) This courage is coming from within the heart. Discovering me has been like digging for precious treasure. I had to accept the fact that I am a sum of all my experiences, good and bad. To be authentic required me to be willing to take responsibility for my life and my choices.

To each of you, I encourage you to allow God to ignite the fire within you and live life intentionally courageous.

Contact Information

Dr. Carolyn Treadwell-Butler PhD, CLC

Website: www.johncmaxwell.com/carolynbutler

e-mail: carolyn@thevisionnavigator.com

Igniting the Fire

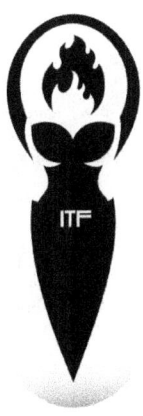

I'm More Than You Think I Am
Kecia Hayslett

Throughout history, and the revelation of what I understand about God, He has used women to accomplish and fulfill many of His strategic purposes in this earth realm. There are many examples and stories in the bible which we can glean from, examples of women taking dangerous risks so that we can have an example of what is possible. I'm convinced that each example and role model adhered to specific attributes, overcame the negative noise and chatter, fear and hindrance in order to overcome and press to the place of their God-ordained destiny. I believe the risks that were taken in the

Igniting the Fire

bible were based on one common risk, and that's the risk that God wants us to take today.

The truth of the matter is that everything we do for God takes a risk, and everything has a cost associated with it via the medium of exchange, our faith. As I read and examine the stories of the courageous women in the Bible, I have to ask myself whether they are taking a risk or a leap of faith.

The Start

"Honey," as I call out to my husband in a certain and uncertain voice. "What would happen if we open the doors to Arms of Compassion Home Care in the month of December? Honey, can we do it? I'm still working full time; however, I want us to be successful entrepreneurs, and I feel this is where God is leading us." I heard nothing for about thirty seconds… silence is golden. I always thought that every moment of every conversation had to be filled with words or sound; he walks softly into the living room

Igniting the Fire

with a stern solider look on his face, no smile, and no facial gestures and replied, "We can start and grow Arms of Compassion together." My emotions are all over the place, scared and happy at the same time. As my heart fills up with excitement, tears roll down my face the size of large rain drops.

I walk to the bathroom, look into the mirror, and I say to the person looking back at me, "Girlfriend, what have you done?" and immediately after I asked myself that question, the negative noise and chatter started. It went something like this, "If I were you, I would not start a business now; you don't know what you are doing--you have no experience in how to start and or grow a business." In my voice of confidence, I replied, "Yes, I can--just watch and see." December 2006, the doors of Arms of Compassion Homecare were open for business.

To my surprise, the current company where I was employed had a client that needed nursing services ASAP. Lawd have mercy, first client intake scheduled for December 1st, 2006. Oh wait, I have no idea how to submit paper work for payment of services rendered, and there are no employees to work. So I did what entrepreneurs do; I became the hired employee to work with the client. I was certain that I was going to have a business, no matter what. Within a matter of 3 weeks, nurses were hired and the client had more than me to care for her.

Has there ever been a time when your intuition was pulling at you and you ignored it or rejected it because you felt you didn't have enough information or education to complete the task, let alone start the task? Well, that was me; my intuition was telling me to seek out some help to grow the business. However, I ignored the inward conversation because of fear of people rejecting me.

The Struggle

The business grows and clients were coming. However, the workloads became challenging, and I found myself putting things off until later and later and later. The negative noise and chatter returned and reminded me of the previous remark, "If I were you, I would not start a business now; you don't know what you are

Igniting the Fire

doing--you have no experience in how to start and or grow a business." and this time the voice added, "You're going to fail, and people are going to laugh at you and regard you as a failure and unsuccessful."

The Process

I admit I started to lose ground and was feeling extremely hopeless. I joined a business networking group searching for assistance and professional guidance, and what I discovered was different people would give me bits and pieces; however, the business continued to spiral down. Sitting in my seat, I was staring out the window and crying so hard that I could hardly breathe or talk.

We came to the realization that we had to close the business down. Even after coming to the decision to close Arms of Compassion Home Care, we still wanted to fight to keep the business open.

Igniting the Fire

Oh God, I have totally made a huge mistake of everything, with debt as deep as the sea and no means to pay it back. We realized that we had to move out of our five-bedroom house, move into an apartment, and find jobs and become employees again. Feeling sorry for myself, I did not want to hear, "I told you so from anybody" so I stayed to myself.

And while staying to myself, the enemy had a party with my mind. He told me that "No one is going to believe in you again," "You are never going to have another business," "You will not have another smile on your face," and "Who's going to forgive you-- are a failure!"

I got so depressed I ran to church and lay prostrate on the altar with my face all in the carpet as often as I could; every time the church doors were open, I was there. Peace is what I was seeking; I desperately wanted to make the pain in my heart to go away. I wanted to have a business that I could pass down to our children and give them a tangible gift that they could grow as they chose.

Igniting the Fire

The Outcome

Prayer and conversations with my husband and mother helped me regain control over my emotions. It doesn't matter how many failures you experience in life; the main thing is to not let the challenge become you. Zig Ziglar reminds us that "Failure is an event not a person." When we allow ourselves to drown in our sorrows, we stop growing--as I was.

The seeds that I planted of growth and success were being pulled up because I thought I failed. Truth is, God is not going to bless whom you pretend to be. So being stripped of everything gave me a chance to reset my thoughts and reconnect with my vision and life. You cannot be fruitful if you're not seed full. In all the pain and vulnerability, there is a seed of faith and expectation that can be planted.

When God unlocks what's in you, He will always do it from a dark place. More truth that has been imbedded in my DNA is that you cannot branch out until you reach in. Are you willing to say

Igniting the Fire

"YES!" to the call that's on your life? Are you willing to be uncomfortable and take a risk? Are you will to be unapologetic about playing full out in life? I challenge you to take a leap of faith with me. JUMP!

Kecia Hayslett

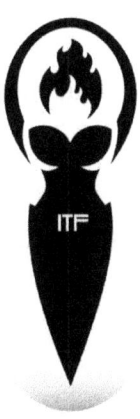

Igniting the Fire

FROM GLOWING ASHES TO PRIMETIME BLAZE
Christy Primmer

It is easy to look at me and see the success I have created. What you do not yet understand is the pain I have endured to get to where I am today.

I am a woman. I am a mother. I am a wife. I am a lover of life. I am a poetic soul. I am a firecracker. I am determined. I am a listening ear. I am tender. I am a fighter. I am a lover. I am a warrior. I am a believer. I am capable and competent. I am that woman who has overcome the uncomfortable chaos, trusting there

Igniting the Fire

is more to life than hiding behind fear. I live unmasked. I am an igniting the fire woman.

The Start

I have always taken great comfort in my work ethic. I over deliver in most things and my career is no exception.

It was fifteen minutes from the time I was told until I handed in my key, passwords, and found myself limping to my car. What had just happened? I could barely breathe. The career that I had used to identify myself as a professional abruptly ended. On the spot. No explanations, just let go. Boom. Everything in my daily routine had just changed in an instant, without any warning.

The Struggle

The worst part of this story was the night before I was fired I had learned that my Dad was given another diagnosis of cancer. I immediately shifted from confident to defeated. In extreme shock

Igniting the Fire

and complete confusion, I cried out, "What else do you think I can possibly handle, Lord?" I sat in my car, wiping the tears away, trying to make sense of it all. I cannot describe in words the gut-wrenching feelings I had in that moment. I had never expected to be fired from a job I was so competent at.

Some of my backstory includes putting incredible pressure on myself to be successful, to blend into the community I'd relocated to for my husband's employment. My family depended on me to provide and to contribute. There I was struggling to process why this was happening to me. I simply could not wrap my mind around it. Needless to say, I felt lost and alone. I felt broken. I had placed way too much value on who I was as a professional and not enough emphasis on the incredible woman I was by nature.

The loss of my professional identity slithered its way into my soul and began to hinder my spiritual growth. It began to eat at me, creating a false sense of who I was: a smart woman with a broken sense of self. I questioned many things and people at that

Igniting the Fire

time in my life. I trusted few. I felt deceived, desperate, and blindsided. Socializing became almost impossible because I wasn't myself; the firecracker, the optimist. How could I have been so naïve? I could not seem to let it go.

I cried a lot, laid in bed for periods of time not wanting to face the world and certainly not wanting to see former colleagues. How would I explain that I'd been fired for reasons I would never know or understand? Can you imagine my embarrassment in having to tell my son why I was not going to work and why I had to put on hold all the luxuries in life I'd been providing him with?

My family doused me with love. My Dad, who had his own struggles, was one of my biggest supporters. An influential man to say the least; he believed in me. My husband reinforced how amazing I was and how we would grow from this, together. He held me when I sobbed, listened when I spoke, and most importantly, provided the safe space for me to sit quietly; if you knew me, you would understand how awkward and odd that was.

Igniting the Fire

Me, quiet? And so it went for a few weeks. Totally out of character, I had sunk into a hole.

The Process

I knew things had to change, and that change would only come through forgiveness of things which I did not understand. I was driving along the highway, music cranked feeling determined, when I began to comprehend the fact that God had not abandoned me, I had abandoned Him. I got lost in prayer and begged Him for a sign of what He had in store for me. I shifted from disappointment and sadness to acceptance and gratitude for the many blessings I had in my life and within my relationships. I had copious amounts of support.

I decided enough was enough. I made a commitment to myself to live by faith and not by fear. I was not one to sit and mope. I'm an action taker. I bounced back; full of inspiration, fuelled with motivation to never leave my self-esteem or financial security in someone else's hands ever again. I realized that God

Igniting the Fire

had much bigger plans for me all along. I needed to stay focused on figuring out how I was going to grow from this experience rather than be defined by it. I started to reclaim my professional identity through integral behavior and decision making. I reached out to former colleagues; all of whom cheered me on and encouraged me to start my own company.

As well educated as I was, I decided to register for school again. University and another piece of paper highlighting my credentials were on the horizon. Losing my job was a blessing in disguise, the best thing that could've ever happened to me. Through the power of my trust in the unknown, I was able to re-focus on speaking my truth and creating the life I had been craving. If I hadn't lost my job, I would have remained stuck at that organization, not fulfilling my true desire. I had always fantasized about running a business but never had the courage to break free from the corporate world or the security of a salary pay check. If I had been searching for a sign, this was it.

The Outcome

Igniting the Fire

I grew determined to no longer feel defeated. I am a natural leader, and everyone knows that leaders seize all opportunities as they come. I was overwhelmed with a soothing sense of calmness that starting my company was precisely what God intended for me to do. The how and what didn't matter yet; it was all about the why, and it was primetime I took action.

It was a dreary morning in November 2011 when I registered my business. Needless to say, the energy shift I experienced was beyond phenomenal. The series of events that happened afterwards were magical, and there were many.

Appreciating life's events takes guts. I dove into action mode and got my hands dirty in all things business. I immediately enjoyed the flexibility I had to spend more time with my Dad while he grew more and more ill. I praised God for the time I was given to be with my mother, to bring light into her life, and to remind her of God's steadfast promise of hope. You see, mindset is what separates the winners from the losers. We must reconcile the fact that we cannot control our destiny; we must have a higher sense of

Igniting the Fire

purpose, no matter what it may be. We need to lean on something to carry us through the dark moments; for me that is faith.

Change is our only guarantee in this lifetime. I realize that even in moments of smoldering darkness God provides glowing ashes which have the potential to light ablaze within. He opened up many doors for me to blossom into the powerhouse that I am today. I reminded myself that I am far more than what others attempt to define me as. I rose above the ashes and ignited the blaze within. I created a business that not only serves my family but also the people I work with. I would never have taken the leap if I wasn't forced to break the cycle I was living. Through a determined mind, soft heart, and plentiful education, I continue to walk through the fires that come my way. I have established financial freedom for myself. I now spend my time teaching others how to refuel and energize their own minds so that they can see their worth in this world. Refueling my connection to faith and trusting that there are reasons for every experience I am gifted

Igniting the Fire

allows me to grow into a better version of myself. Faith is my invisible security blanket, always there and never abandoning me.

I leave you with the knowledge that no matter where you've been or where you are, you can get to where you're going, and you don't have to do it alone. There is a divine source of intelligence at work in your life; tune in to it and create the life you desire. The power is within you.

Christy Primmer

Primetime Consulting Services

www.primetimecs.com

Igniting the Fire

EMPOWERED TO TRIUMPH!

Rev. Diana R. Williams

It is exciting to be a woman who is now a part of this next God movement of greater works, deeper revelations, promises fulfilled, and opened doors. We are women who are also daughters, wives, mothers, grandmothers, sisters, aunts, and nieces. We are single women who have never been married or women who are single again through divorce or widowhood. We are women who work inside or outside of the

Igniting the Fire

home in business or civic leadership. We are nurturers who are seasoned with age and experience. And finally, we are anointed women who have answered the glorious call to ministry while juggling many roles!

The Start

My call story starts a few years after my rebirth encounter with the Lord. It wasn't until I was a young woman with my life in shambles that I began a personal relationship with the Lord. After two years of marriage to my college sweetheart, I was a frazzled mother of an active girl toddler on my way to divorce court. Thankfully, this new intimacy with the Lord ignited a hunger and thirst within me for the Word. I started each day reading the Bible and began attending worship and Bible study in earnest. After inviting my husband to church and his subsequent rebirth experience, we reconciled, not knowing that God had plans for me to embark on the marvelous journey of ministry service.

Igniting the Fire

The Struggle

What happened next shattered my world and everything I had constructed about how God faithfully moves in the life of people. Doubled over in pain with severe cramping and heavy hemorrhaging, the ER doctor confirmed that I was losing our new baby and would need a surgical procedure. Through that dark night, I slipped in and out of consciousness with the question "*WHY*?" ringing in my heart. My soul and empty womb cried out for the Lord's comfort and in time, I began to heal physically and emotionally. This early life lesson in suffering and disappointment equipped me with a personal testimony of encouragement wrought through firsthand experience.

After the miscarriage and my crisis of faith, I answered my call to ministry understanding that God was doing a new thing in my life. Meanwhile, our family grew to include two more daughters, a son, then another daughter. As a mother of five children, simultaneously I experienced the hectic teenaged years, adolescence, late elementary, early elementary and pre-school years. Juggling many hats at once all while serving in ministry, I became a licensed evangelist, boldly going wherever God sent me.

Another pivotal point in ministry happened when our daughter tried to end her life. She was fifteen years old, in the tenth grade and madly in love with an eighteen year old senior. Our daughter was exhibiting incidents of teenage rebellion and the "preacher's kid" syndrome. Everything erupted one Saturday evening when I got a phone call from the young man whom I saw as the culprit for all of her bad choices. He told me that she had just called him and said that she took pills to kill herself. I screamed for my husband, and we raced upstairs to her locked bedroom. After breaking the door open, my husband picked her up, and we raced to the emergency room. She was lethargic but conscious as we arrived at the hospital in what seemed like an alternate reality where everything moved in slow motion.

Once we got to triage and they gave her a charcoal substance to induce vomiting, I found out that she had taken a hand full of Tylenol. The doctors felt that she did not take enough pills

Igniting the Fire

to end her life, but the danger was the potential for liver damage. Clearly this was all a big mistake or a horrible nightmare! If only we could turn back the clock to the day before when our beautiful daughter headed out to school without a care in the world. So many thoughts ran through my mind that night. Was this a cry for help, or did our daughter despair because she had lost all hope?

The next day she was released from the hospital in my care. Normally, when a teenager attempts suicide, she has to stay in the hospital's psychiatric ward under observation for three days. This requirement was waived because I am clergy and agreed to follow-up with a licensed counselor the next day. We may never understand why an increasing number of people of all ages, diverse backgrounds and social standing opt out of life. The reasons may be varied, but the piercing outcome remains the same. It is a tragedy when pain and despair cause anyone to decide that life is no longer worth living. Once it is done, the person who chooses self-annihilation can never take it back.

Igniting the Fire

After the initial shock wore off, we had to deal with the implications of our daughter's suicide attempt, and I had to take a closer look at how I served God in my own household. Ironically, one of my duties as a full-time associate pastor of a large urban church with over 4,000 members was to oversee the ministries that interfaced with family and women's issues. This included pastoral care and counseling as well as initial grief counseling to parishioners. If I could not see what was brewing within my own family, how could I expect to serve effectively at my charge? This was a crisis of ministry for me, a crisis of health for the family, and a personal crisis of self-worth for our daughter.

The Process

My soul cried out in anguish because one of the things told to women in ministry who have families is that our families will be ruined for a lack of attention on our part. I was consumed with guilt, burned out, discouraged, and emotionally exhausted as I re-examined my ministry vocation. Was this really the cost for saying

Igniting the Fire

yes to ministry? Was God still with me or was God displeased with me? Did my daughter almost lose her life because I had somehow made a mistake years ago about what God was requiring of me?

Through deep reflection on my part of the nature of God and my relationship with the Lord, the heaviness lifted. The God I encountered in this crisis of ministry was the God that drew me close and shielded me with loving kindness. It was a time of refreshing that required unshakable faith and audacious hope to face the unchartered territory and shattered pieces of our lives. Even though I cried many tears and experienced emotions that ranged from acute sadness to righteous indignation, the promises of God faithfully kicked in. Weeping endured for a period of night, but renewed joy unspeakable came in the morning! I knew for certain that this was spiritual warfare against which God's favor surrounded me and my family as a shield and protected us. What could have gone another way, God turned around supernaturally and used to inform another level of encouragement in my ministry mandate! What looked like defeat was a spring board to higher levels and deeper dimensions of victory!

The Outcome

There are many other situations I could share that seemed as if defeat was imminent. Yet, in every circumstance God sent a mighty breakthrough, *"For God has said, I will not in any way fail you nor give you up nor leave you without support. I will not in any degree leave you helpless nor forsake you nor let you down nor relax My hold on you! Assuredly not!"* Hebrews 13: b, Amplified.

My passion is now sharing with others how to triumph over temporary low periods in life. I have spent years in prayer and extensively studying the Bible searching for biblical strategies to overcome difficult and painful challenges. These are lessons that I apply to my personal life, my marriage of almost 43 years, parenting, grand parenting, and within my ministry. The books I have written (Help to Get Over It, Get Out of The Dry Places, and

Igniting the Fire

You Are Set Apart And Transformed), and The New Sound of Triumph CD are all informed by these lessons learned to inspire others.

My Praise Portfolio is full of testimonies of what I know God will do! The Master of Divinity I received in 2011 awarded dual concentrations in Religion, Health and Science and in Women and Religion. Currently, I am enrolled in a doctoral program for Educational Leadership in Christian Ministry. Throughout my ministry I have developed a deep compassion for health issues and problems around childbirth for which numerous women have sought my counsel! All five of my children are married with children of their own, and today that daughter is a thirty-one year old wife and mother who is serving the Lord! The ecclesial authority in which I now walk is God-given, God-inspired, and God-empowered!

"Now thanks be unto God, which always causeth us to triumph in Christ!"
2 Corinthians 2:14a, KJV

Igniting the Fire

By Rev. Diana R. Williams, M. Div.

Chief Encouragement Overseer

Declaring Righteousness Worldwide Ministries

& Encouragement Consulting - *DRWMEC*

www.RevDianaRWilliams.com

RESTORED, REBOOTED, REVIVED... RELEVANT ME

Dr. Nekeshia C. Doctor

Dr. Nekeshia C. Doctor is a daughter, sister, granddaughter, aunt, cousin, niece, wife, parent, and Christian. She is an educator of fifteen years who is zealous about coaching, mentoring, and supporting parents, youth, and educators to excel at their highest potential and obtain unlimited possibilities. She empowers youth from various walks of life to identify who they are, embrace who they were divinely created to be, love themselves first, and stand in their own brilliance.

Igniting the Fire

Dr. Nekeshia C. Doctor is CEO of JALIA Consulting, Inc. where she is an Educational Consultant and Leadership Coach who provides consulting services for parent/youth and executive leaders/staff on how to impact youth and get desired results in homes or organizations. Her ability to empower others and build a positive culture within any household or organization speaks for itself. She is also Founder/Executive Director of The BW Project, Inc., and a 501(c) 3 nonprofit organization that focuses on self-empowerment, self-confidence, self-sufficiency, leadership, and respect. It is tailored to girls between the ages of 8-18 years old. Dr. Doctor is an active member of Delta Sigma Theta Sorority, Inc.

In this chapter, Dr. Doctor shares her own story that involves personal challenges and uncertainties as a young girl. Despite being the eldest daughter, she wrestled with her own internal and external beauty. After years of silent struggles with her self-esteem, she found ways to escape the internal battle with self. She discovered her relevance through a transformation of her mindset, a self-love support system, and the right tools in place to break

Igniting the Fire

through that glass ceiling of fear and unworthiness. Dr. Doctor believes that life is about conquering our social inhibitions and extending a hand to help and bless others who may share those same fears.

The Start

As the firstborn daughter of a teen mother, I was raised in a single-parent home until I was 10 years old with loving support from my mother and family. When I was 10 years old, my mother married my "Pops," my amazing stepfather who accepted my sister and me as his own biological daughters. Although we received and felt love in our family growing up, I discerned a difference from others as I grew older. I took notice of how family, friends, and even strangers would treat my sister and me differently.

My sister had the golden-brown skin tone, plump cute cheeks with dimples, and nice, thick legs that people always complimented in such a jovial way. They would make comments such as "She is adorable. She is so pretty with those cute, little dimples." However,

Igniting the Fire

I have a pecan, dark-brown skin tone, long structured facial features, and beautiful course hair, but my compliments never matched those given to my sister. Others would notice me and simply say, "You look just like your mother."

As a child, it would make me smile to hear that because I resemble my beautiful mother. Yet, at the time it still felt different compared to how people responded to my baby sister

The Struggle

Although I felt special to my mother and family, I often felt as though I was a mistake and burden because I was the by-product of a 15-year old teenager who was still a child herself. Despite any odds, my mother and Pops took pride in raising me and my sister. They never treated us differently or demonstrated any favoritism. If my mother ever noticed that others treated us differently, she would address it.

Regardless of my parent's love and protection, the mental and emotional battle that I had within me grew. I did not feel attractive

Igniting the Fire

because I felt others did not find me beautiful or appealing. As a teenager, I was shy and a bit withdrawn from others unless I felt that I could trust someone. I had difficulty accepting compliments from peers and adults because I was unsure if they were genuine. I had grown accustomed to my sister receiving all of the compliments. So, when someone did recognize me, I did not know how to accept it. I had friendships that I valued, but would only allow friends to get so close to me. This was my way of protecting my heart and shielding my feelings of unwanted hurt and rejection. On March 8, 1992, I accepted Jesus Christ as Lord and Savior of my life at the age of 15 because I wanted to rid myself of this battle within my mind.

I came to understand that He was my help in the time of trouble and would hide me in His secret place. Considering that He is not a physical being, I trusted Him to not hurt me. I asked God to change my heart and do something new in me.

As a young lady in my early 20's, I recall still struggling with identifying my self-worth and purpose in life. I felt worthless, as

Igniting the Fire

though I had no relevance on this earth. I found myself trying to compensate for my own insecurities by making others happy and keeping them laughing. I have always enjoyed serving and helping others, which allowed me to take my mind off of how I felt about myself. Inspiring others, no matter the age, came naturally for me, but I rarely could empower myself and discover my purpose in life and thrive.

The Process

One day, after receiving a thoughtful gift from my mother, I had an awakening, and it changed my life. It changed my life because my way of thinking shifted. The gift my mother gave me was a picture of a lion looking at itself in the mirror with a quote that stated, **"YOU ARE YOUR ONLY LIMITATION."** As a way to help transform my thinking, I would keep this picture on my desk in my classroom and office as a school administrator. I chose to do this to not only inspire me daily, but my students as well. I wanted to empower them to take the limits off of themselves and aim high.

Igniting the Fire

This became one of my first personal affirmations that I declared out of my mouth every day as a reminder to keep going no matter what and that if I stopped, then I've defeated myself. I would have no one to blame or give credit to negative energy, but ME. Over time, I realized that I have the POWER to speak or think life over death by the words I choose to speak out of my mouth and thoughts I choose to give energy to and allow to take up space in my mind. We can only progress in life as far as we allow ourselves to. I believe that our level of prosperity and success in life is predicated by us individually and the limits we place on our lives. I overcame my social inhibitions by declaring daily affirmations over my life such as "I AM a designer's original.

I AM beautiful and matter in this world." Then, I created a daily regimen to continue self-empowerment. You see, one has to want it, want more, want greater, and I did. I was ready to transform from "stuck in a rut" to "ALIVE and THRIVING." My daily regimen is what I call my **"P.O.W.E.R."** prescription. My daily dosage empowers me to:

Igniting the Fire

P- Practice loving myself daily; push until I see results.

O- Open my eyes and ears to whom God created me to be.

W- Walk it out; stay the course even when the going gets tough.

E- Elevate my thinking and how I see myself.

R- Realize that there is greatness inside of me; I run with the herd that is going in the same direction.

The Outcome

Throughout the course of my struggles, I still experienced some triumph. It was earning my Doctorate degree in Education that allowed others to see that my teenage mother's journey and choice to keep and raise me were not mistakes. Today, my passion, life, and work as an educator, mentor, and Founder of a 501(c)3 nonprofit organization, are all about opening new windows of possibility for girls and women who have been challenged by their staggered mindsets and choices and who are seeking a path to make the most of their lives. I am able to say today that I am FREE

Igniting the Fire

of mental and emotional bondage. I have the power aligned with a courageous mind and spirit to take on the world and never look back, but to use my past struggles as a stepping stone to go higher.

For every girl and woman across this world, from all walks of life, who has been told and made to feel as though she is a mistake, hear this. No matter what others have said and may continue to utter —no matter how many times you have fallen off course, no matter how little support and love you have surrounding you, you can BE and DO anything that you desire to BE and DO. **As you discover your brilliance, EMBRACE it, OWN it, and STAND in it with no apologies.**

Dr. Nekeshia C. Doctor

www.jaliaconsulting.com/ www.thebwproject.org

Igniting the Fire

ME BY DEFINITION
Tiffany L. Hutchins, MS. LPC

Strength is a word that my friends today would probably use to define me. However, I've always been good at hiding because in my house where the story begins, you didn't show your feelings, you were told your feelings. This is a story of defining me, exploring me, and loving me. There have been a lot of heartbreaks, but one word stands out about how I would define me, **TRIUMPHANT.**

Igniting the Fire

I truly believe that the trials you are about to read were specifically meant for me in order to become the person I am and walk in the purpose that God has for my life. The story ends with me. Today, I choose strength. I choose faith. I choose myself. My story is ongoing; it doesn't stop with the conclusion because my story of overcoming is still being written today as I choose daily to define myself in Christ.

The Start

The innocence and naivety that consumed me in my young age about what life was not is the kind of life that every parent dreams their kids will have with no harm, no hurt, and no pain. I was the typical 90's kid and teenager. I was a straight "A" student and athlete, and I generally got along with my new classmates at my new high school.

I loathed the strictness of my father, but high school friends, track meets, and the Dairy Queen gave me refuge. The shift in my life

Igniting the Fire

began in my early teen years. I was being exposed to more of "the world," and life was beginning to hit me in a way that would change my life forever.

The Struggle

Unwanted. Unloved. Confused. These are words I would use to describe how I felt during most of my childhood. My parents were divorced, and I couldn't understand why I had to go and visit my mother every other weekend when most kids in my same situation visited their fathers. Unfortunately for me, looking exactly like my mother didn't go over well for me. I felt like I had a sign over my head that said, **"HISTORY REPEATS ITSELF."**

You see, my mother had me when she was 17, and it seemed like that's all my father could see in me, my mother's daughter, who was destined to become a teen mother. To me, my mother was my hero, the person I aspired to be like, and there was nothing that

Igniting the Fire

anyone could say to make me change my mind. So I rebelled. As I got older, I got angrier. I hated everyone.

I hated myself. I just wanted to get away from this fucking place. But even getting away didn't change anything; I was happier when I was away, but things that no child should ever have to worry about happened to me when I was away. Things I kept secret because I was an outcast. Who would believe me?

Then it happened; my whole world was changed. One call on August 6th, 2000 changed who I was. I lost my high school sweetheart. My best friend was taken from my by a drunk driver, and although my friends tried to console me and my parents tried to rationalize, I was never to be the same again. I spent much of the rest of my high school years wishing to be away, wishing to be dead, wishing to be anyone else other than Tiffany.

Needless to say, after graduation and on to college, and my experiences of unfortunate events continued at a rapid rate. I realized that I hadn't learned to be social. The strictness of my home life in high school prevented me from hanging out past

Igniting the Fire

school hours, or going to sleepovers or social gatherings outside of sports that I was a part of and field trips. Happiness was a thing that my heart just could not understand.

I longed for acceptance and love; I often felt alone. Friends that I had made were dropping off the radar, and I blamed it mostly on my social awkwardness and lack of "personality," but some of these friends were just not good for me, and I was too naïve to see it.

I found alcohol a comforting friend I would drink before class, during class, and after class. I wanted to be numb. It was easy; no one noticed and no one cared enough to realize that I was an alcoholic. Again, I was good at hiding. Ultimately, even my friend in alcohol became my enemy. I was raped. In my alcoholic stupor on a night out with a girlfriend I really barely knew, we were invited to a party.

Was it strange that this party was just me, her, and two guys? Of course. Did I notice? I was too drunk to even know what my name was. He took something that didn't belong to him and left me to pick up the pieces. This was my secret. This was my fault, so why should I tell anyone. I deserved it.

My days went on as if nothing ever happened. I continued marking the days off the calendar until graduation. I had succeeded on the outside, but on the inside, I wanted it all to end. I wanted to kill myself.

The Process

There has always been a strong sense of tunnel vision when it comes to my goals and dreams. I knew I wanted to be a pediatrician at a young age, and when chemistry became a personal obstacle for me, I quickly found another field in which I could help others.

When I became pregnant, on a collision course with single motherhood, and was forced to move home, my eyes and thoughts remained on the vision. I finally figured out in a grad school counseling class that the problem was that I was waiting on others

Igniting the Fire

to define who I was and I was allowing my traumas define me instead of defining myself for myself and in the eyes of God.

It was at that point that I decided to choose me. I started therapy and found my love for writing through journaling. It was like I could tell someone what I was feeling without having to actually tell anyone. Of course, with choosing me, I had to choose a different mindset. Easier said than done. Being a single mother was definitely not in the plans.

I had graduated with my Masters and was finally on the road to getting my PhD in Atlanta, Ga. This was a roadblock that I wasn't ready for. It was difficult to see myself beyond this point. I kept thinking to myself, "Oh great, another label." Giving up was never an option; I just had to find another way to "skin the cat."

I planned for the day I would move out of my parents' home and begin my PhD, and when tunnel vision kicked in for me again, with motivation from my little one, and the support of family and friends, there was no stopping me.

The Outcome

Igniting the Fire

Sometimes things happen to us, and there is no way that we could have done anything, and nothing that we could have said, and no other way we could have handled it for that to change. Other times, we happen to ourselves. We get in our own way, and we overstep God's process and timing for our lives. Life may have been different if some of my choices had been different. I learned to find peace with my position.

We must own our positions. Whether by our choices or by praying for a position we thought we were ready for, at this point in our lives we were meant to be exactly where we are. We must evaluate our position. Take the time to look at where you are, who you are, and who you have in your life. If you don't like it, change it. Don't wait on someone to give you permission. You have the power to change your life.

I make the decision still today that I will be in peace with the position that I am currently in and that I will not let my past or

Igniting the Fire

others define who Tiffany is. I have never been so triumphant and proud to be Tiffany. Three years ago I started a journey to finalize my academic career. I am now only a few short months from walking the stage for the final time and adding Dr. in front of my name.

I am the owner of two businesses and the mother of a spirited 4 year old. I get to wake up every day and help those who have lost hope find strength and peace that they've never had before. I get to give the lessons that I have learned about self-love to others and foster strength like never before.

Most importantly, I trust God. I trust in the timing that He has for my life and that the vision He gave me when I was just 14 is still the purpose that He has for my life.

Tiffany L. Hutchins, MS. LPC

www.trinitygiveshope.com

Igniting the Fire

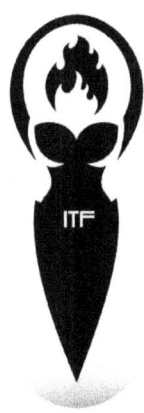

BLESSED IS SHE WHO BELIEVED...

Nakilah Shannon

Opening

I am a Daughter of the Most High. I am fearfully and wonderfully made. It's who I was even when I didn't believe it. It's who I've always been. Before the babies, bad choices, and horrible relationships, I was a Daughter of the Most High. My story is about me believing that I was who God said I was and the blessings that followed.

Igniting the Fire

The Start

For as far back as I could remember, I knew I was different. I grew up in the "hood" but had a different mindset and mentality. I liked different types of things than my friends did. I always found myself trying to figure out who I was. I did not quite fit in.

I grew up in church. Every time the doors of the church opened, we were there. That is when I begin to fall in love with God. The music would move me to tears even when I did not know what I was crying about. The preacher talking about this loving God kept me at the edge of my seat. I would see the people shouting and "catching the Holy Ghost," and after the giggling stopped, I decided in my heart that I wanted to do the same. I believed that shouting and tarrying to "catch the Holy Ghost" was what I needed to do to be close to God and to begin to fulfill the purpose of my life.

As a young girl in my early teens, I would lie in the bed and talk to God. We would spend hours just chatting about my day and what

Igniting the Fire

was going on. We were building our relationship. I believed He loved me and I loved Him. I would have visions of being on stage speaking to thousands and thousands of people, stadiums full. It was at that time that God begin to reveal to me the purpose He had for my life. I realized that God would use me to speak to people. I was not sure exactly WHAT He would have me share, but I figured it would be something important if that many people showed up. It was in those moments that I begin to understand a little better about where I belonged.

The Struggle

It was also during this time that I found myself struggling with my religious identity as well. I knew I loved God, and I knew He loved me. There was not a doubt in my mind about it. What I did have a problem with was Jesus. The denomination I belonged to at that time believed that the evidence of being "saved" was speaking in tongues. Being very young and immature in the faith, I begin to realize that unless I spoke in tongues, I would not be able to be with God the way that I wanted. I believed that since it was a "gift"

Igniting the Fire

and the only way to the Father is through the Son Jesus, that it was Jesus who would give me the gift of speaking in tongues.

I begin to beg Jesus to give me the gift. Every Sunday I would pray that today would be the day Jesus would be so generous and bless me with the gift to speak in tongues. I would tarry in secret and go to the altar in hopes of catching it while I was there for prayer. It never happened.

I was never able to speak in tongues, so I believed that Jesus was being selfish and for whatever reason was withholding this gift from me. In my church you could not serve outside of being in the choir unless you had received the gift of tongues.

So at this point, I was heartbroken because Jesus had not given me the gift and now I can't serve God. Just as I was beginning to learn my purpose and understand who I was in God, Jesus was taking away that opportunity. This is when I begin to stray away from the church. I was finally of age to make my decisions about if I would go to church or not, and I chose not to. I stopped going to church,

Igniting the Fire

and eventually I felt being with God would be impossible. This is when I began to turn my back on Jesus and decided I wanted nothing to do with Him. I was hurt and angry.

I spent my time in college studying every religion other than Christianity. I knew it said there was only one way to the Father, but I was bound and determined to find another way to God. I believed there could be many paths to God, and I did not have to go through Jesus to get to Him. It was during this period that my life began to fall apart.

I found myself in a relationship that was not beneficial to me at all. He wanted to love me but he did not know how. He did not even know how to love himself. I was living below my potential, and I was falling into a depression. Although God was keeping me through this period, I was still very far away from Him.

I did not know myself, my value or my worth. When I was not in my primary destructive relationship, I was in secondary relationships wasting my time and life. I was leaving a trail of hurt feelings and breaking my own heart and spirit in the process.

I was barely 25 and had my second child and was living the life of a 45 year old. I was working full time and going to school and trying to play the wife and raise my children. I was doing all of this under my own strength. I was also doing this not knowing who I was and what I wanted to do with my life. I had pushed my dreams that I shared with God to the wayside. I no longer saw myself as being a mouthpiece for God. I was miserable. I was not a good mother, I was having suicidal thoughts, and I was giving my body away and mistreating my heart in the process.

The Process

I wish I could say one day I woke up and decided to make a change for the better. I had some better moments when I decided I would leave my long standing relationship alone. I packed up the kids and moved with very little warning. I promised God I would not go back to it if He just got me out. All I did was leave that relationship and go to several mini-toxic relationships. I was still

Igniting the Fire

angry at Jesus and did not know where to turn or who I had become.

I remember waking up on a Sunday morning and hearing the voice of God. He simply said, "That's enough," and I knew it was time to get myself together. He instructed me to go to the church where my baby was in daycare. I had not been to church in years. I did not know what to expect or what God had in store for me. I just knew I was tired, lonely, hurt, used and abused. I did not know who I was and did not understand why God would even bother to care about me.

When I began to go to the church, it was clear to me what I had been missing. Under the teaching of the Pastor and the hands on Bible study, I was able to learn for myself about salvation and who Jesus really was. I realized that He loved me and would never withhold God from me. I was also able to see a woman Pastor, which was very new to me. I was able to see God <u>use a woman to lead His people and to share His Word with others.</u>

Igniting the Fire

The Outcome

It was during this time that I also begin to find who I was as well. A leader began to spring forth within me. I discovered how much God loved me and that Jesus desired a relationship with me as well. It was during this time that God begin to heal me and restore me. It was during this time I accepted my call to the ministry and I birthed **"Hagar's Fountain of Hope"** ministry. God allowed me to go through everything I went through for a reason. I was not just a church girl but a woman who CHOSE Jesus. We had a relationship and not something forced through religion.

I was developing into a woman of God who was coming into her place as a Daughter of the Most High. God has done AMAZING things in my life. He's birthed books, ministries, business, and allowed me to be a blessing to others. Blessed is she who has believed that the Lord would fulfill His promises to her (Luke 1:48)! Do you believe?

Nakilah Shannon

Igniting the Fire

Igniting the Fire

Igniting the Fire

FINDING LOVE FROM THE INSIDE OUT
Phillis Shimamoto

I was born and raised in a typical American family in Southern California. We ate hamburgers, hot dogs, apple pie and spaghetti. There were three girls: my twin sister, my younger sister who was born four years behind us, and me. The two things that differentiated me from everyone else at school were my almond eyes and Japanese heritage; I hated both and would've given *anything* to be Caucasian.

Historically, Japanese people are stoic, stern and rigid, rarely speak much, show little emotion and believe in loyalty, honor, respect, ethics and integrity. Dad told us outright that we

Igniting the Fire

should never bring shame to the family by ruining the family name. It wouldn't be tolerated. As a young girl, Dad's inability to show affection bothered me greatly. I would sob in mom's arms, looking for solace, but completely devastated and crushed emotionally. Being greeted by silence most of the time seemed to be the norm. I wanted and needed validation and assurance that I was loved and longed to hear the words: *I love you.* "What did I do wrong to make Dad so mad at me that he couldn't and wouldn't tell me that he loved me? How could I get a gauge on his emotions when he didn't communicate and show much emotion at all?" These questions danced in my head all the time.

The Start

Dad's strict and inflexible ways felt confining, and I rebelled often. Our relationship seemed to worsen as I went through my teen years. Our communication deteriorated, and my defensive wall went up. Dad often felt cold and distant. I withdrew as my anger, rage and resentment grew. Whenever I chose to voice my opinion, I was promptly cut off in mid-sentence. Not seen and

Igniting the Fire

rarely heard. The silence was so palpable, and I yearned to be able to have a voice, but learned quickly that the best way to keep the peace was to keep quiet and behave. My perception was that Dad didn't really love me, so I developed perfectionist and overachiever tendencies. My thought was that I would "earn" his love by achieving and excelling and would get his attention in this manner.

At the age of eight or nine, my twin sister and I started to encounter bullying at school. The horrible racial slurs of "Jap" were so painful and hurtful that I was crushed to my core. It was like pouring salt on already raw wounds. I never knew when the bullies would verbally attack me on the playground or the hallways, so my guard was always up, and I did whatever I could to avoid them at all cost. My younger sister and cousins experienced the same thing, too. Mired in angst and stress all of the time because of things going on at home and school, my stomach was always in knots, and I was sick often. My fragile body was so riddled with anxiety that restless and sleepless nights ensued

Igniting the Fire

throughout my school years. Ironically, I wanted attention, but not the kind that I got from the bullies. I shied away and shunned the spotlight and kept withdrawing, keeping all of my real feelings buried deep inside. The relentless onslaught and barrage of racial epithets such as "Jap" and "You're stupid, dumb, and ugly and you'll never amount to anything" kept coming. I'd yell back and plug my ears with my fingers, shaking my head as if to wish the hurt away. Words were silent killers to me; meanwhile, I was seething.

I suffered greatly from very low self-esteem and self-confidence. I became a people pleaser with hopes of being liked, valued, loved and accepted. I didn't want anything to do with my heritage, but the underlying shame was always present even though I was never cognizant of it.

Dad experienced the shame of being in the Japanese internment camp for 3 ½ years after Japan bombed Pearl Harbor, despite having been born in San Diego, and the same generational shame trickled down to me as I dealt with bullying.

Igniting the Fire

I angrily thought to myself, "Why do I have to be Japanese?" And with anger brewing, I'd repeat the words, "I hate being Japanese, I hate it!" Nothing good had been associated with my heritage, and things just seemed to be getting progressively worse.

The Struggle

I continued sleepwalking through life. There had been little inner happiness, joy or sparkle, only sadness, loneliness and a huge vacancy in my heart. No one was home or had been home for years! I was the master of disguise at hiding my shame. The time had come to stop pretending that life was great and to stop running from myself.

The Process

Over the years, I remained a victim, blaming Dad and the bullies for what had transpired and for the way I felt about myself until I took full responsibility for my life at age 47. Five years ago, I finally looked in the mirror one morning and angrily shouted,

Igniting the Fire

"Who in the hell are you?" I answered silently, "I don't even know....." and I broke down in loud muffled sobs. That was the breaking point for me.

Exposing my insecurities and learning to tap into my emotions was so difficult and scary. No longer willing to keep up the façade and finally admitting that under that perfect persona that I had masterfully created was a very fragile, broken and shattered little girl. Finally, speaking my truth had set me free.

The Outcome

Out of complete vulnerability, rawness, buckets of tears and facing my own uncomfortableness has come wholeness of self. When I said "yes" to me, it was the first act of self-love that I had ever really given myself. What a gift! Now I know the most important relationship each of us will ever have is the relationship that we have with ourselves.

I felt that Dad owed me an acknowledgement and apology, but I've come to realize that Dad owes me nothing. He did his job

Igniting the Fire

by raising us and doing the very best that he knew how, and the way that he showed love and support was by providing for our family and attending all of our school activities.

In my mind, though, love wasn't "doing" something; it was "showing" it physically because that's what my sensitive soul needed growing up. However, Dad wasn't capable of showing the kind of love I wanted based on his cultural upbringing. It's taken years, but Dad and I have reached a common ground and an amicable understanding.

Releasing and letting go of the anger, resentment and bitterness was a process for me, and when I could let go of the final strand of those pent up emotions, it allowed me to appreciate what a wonderful man and humanitarian Dad really is -- someone who worked tireless in his community for decades, so why change him?

I've learned that it's not my business to change him, just as it's not his business to change me. We can be ourselves, knowing

Igniting the Fire

that where we are now is where we're always meant to be…but in God's time and in His way.

I kept praying that God would soften my heart and that I would be able to forgive Dad and release the negatively-charged feelings that I had harbored inside of me. I think God knew that my heart had to be fully open, that I had to evolve and grow as a person before forgiveness could happen with Dad and before I could forgive myself.

Plagued by always feeling inadequate and not good enough, I took on and carried around the "life sentence" of the bullies. Self-imprisonment didn't allow me to be anyone else until I finally woke up to myself.

Every experience, however traumatic, taught me a lesson and to have an even deeper level of compassion for myself and others. I found the connection and love that I was looking for all along: love for myself.

Igniting the Fire

You see, love has no boundaries. Society sets those boundaries, and our parents reinforce them. It's up to each of us to live outside the box we are put in while loving and honoring ourselves in the process.

Who says we have to live within the confines of rules? Rules and circumstances don't have to define us. Look within and be honest with yourself to find your own truth, to live fully and in integrity with yourself and live passionately and on purpose. Hiding and playing small serves no one and is a huge disservice to the world. Love is always an inside job because love is not found outside of us through other people, but solely within our own heart.

Today I live freely, peacefully and proudly and in alignment with my own truth, passion, purpose and calling. I thank God for my life. My heart is full, and I continually remind myself to live consciously and to look within. Truth is *always* found there.

Phillis Shimamoto

Instructor, Speaker & Transformational Life Educator

Igniting the Fire

www.PhillisShimamoto.com

AGAINST ALL ODDS...YOU CAN BE AN OVERCOMER!

Pastor Michelle A Broadnax

Hello Sister-Friends!

Thank you for allowing me to share a part of my journey with you. My prayer is that through my story, if it finds you in a place of hardship, doubt, or despair, your fire would be reignited and your hope in God rekindled. If you are a non-believer, I pray it will be a testament to you that God is real!

Igniting the Fire

The Start

In writing this book, I realized there were important episodes in my life that significantly shaped my life, as a child, teen and young woman. It would be my first episode that would prove to prevail against all odds. That night at eight years old, I had my first encounter with God, where he told me, "You will always need to speak to Me."

The Struggle

Shortly following that encounter, life dealt some harsh blows to that little eight year old girl who would be faced with grown up issues; she learned to keep secrets in the night and had to endure things a child shouldn't even have to think about; now that Pandora's box was opened…living with a mask would become her way of survival!

Igniting the Fire

By the eighth grade, I had learned how to put on a mask, using substances and alcohol. I had absolutely no understanding of how to cope with my emotions. ... In search of love and acceptance, I ran into wall after wall, abusive man after abusive man.

Then I would face a betrayal that would change my life. My closest cousin and her mom broke my heart. She stole my first boyfriend, and when I told my aunt, she basically told me I wasn't worthy of him. I was very angry and hurt at what they had done, and to add insult to injury, one day my cousin visited my high school with my ex-boyfriend's sister. I became enraged at how she just didn't care about me or my feelings. Not knowing how to deal with my rage, addictions, and secrets... I lost it. I charged at her with everything I had and smacked the life out of her; I hit her so hard, her earrings flew off! All you could hear from the students was "Oooooo!"

By the time I got home, every family member in town seemed to be at my house, ready to get me. But my mother stood up for me and would not allow them to touch me. There I was, fifteen years

Igniting the Fire

old, with my heart shattered again. I felt no one cared about me or the pain she had caused me as she flaunted herself around town with my "man." After that incident, I felt very distant from my blood relatives; it was a tear that never mended.

During my transition from youth into womanhood, I was angry; I was traumatically scarred several times over, and I had no family except my mother. Then another tragedy hit -- I lost my mother to colon cancer. I was devastated! There I was, seven months pregnant with my third son at twenty-one, and my only advocate, my only safe place, was taken from me.

My mom and I were so close; I could talk to her about everything. I remember when I had my first son at eighteen; my dad would come into the room, only to find my mom holding my son in one arm, and me in the other.

He would scream, "Michelley, get off her!" and I would respond, "No, she was my mom before his grandmother." Mom never

Igniting the Fire

seemed to mind. She would hold me and let me sit on her for as long as I wanted.

The night she passed, they had told me she had another two months to live, so I didn't need to come by. That day I wrote her a letter to share with her all about our times together. See, as the cancer progressed, she started to forget who I was. I wanted to remind her of all the wonderful times we shared. It wasn't until the day of her wake that I would able to read that letter.

The night I lost her was another blow to my already fragile mind. Picture me arriving at the hospital seven months pregnant at 3 am, because for the first time in months, I let my friends convince me to go out. As I walked down the long hospital corridor, someone whispered, "That's her daughter."

When I got her room, they pulled the curtain back, and there she was; she looked so peaceful and yet so lifeless. I thrust myself onto her body, holding her like I had so many times before, but then my

Igniting the Fire

father in his own pain began to cuss and scream at me for going out.

Dad and I never got along; we always fought, but this was not the time. I could not take it. I jumped up and began cussing back at him, screaming I would kill him. I was quickly rushed out the room.

Three months later, I had my last son, and soon after, I tried to take my life…A few years later my brother succeeded by hanging himself at our mom's grave. After that I no longer allowed suicide to be an option out.

Through all of those great tragedies, the thing that kept me going was my encounter with God!

The Process

So, what ultimately healed me? How was I delivered with no women in my life to teach me how to be a woman or a mother? No

Igniting the Fire

mentors to encourage me? No rehabs or groups? Simple, it was God's love for me. While I was out searching for love, True Love was in hot pursuit of me... but I was too broken to turn around and notice.

God's loving grace and the gift he gave me to help other women is what broke me free from the deception of all that false love offered. Helping others became my personal healing grace.

You see, the things I wanted to hear someone say to me, I began to speak over other women. That is what I now call, "The Boomerang Effect." When I spoke life to someone else, I would see something in their eyes change, a glimpse of hope, and a belief that they could be more, even if for just a brief moment.

Watching her body language change, as her shoulders would rise and her chin would lift up! It was, and is the most precious sight to see -- when the love of God comes through you, and imparts a seed of hope to someone who thought there was no hope. When I would see the effect it had on others...it caused me to put my shoulders

Igniting the Fire

back, lift my head a little higher, and there it was, "The Boomerang Effect"!

Learning how to overcome the victim mentality and how to deal with my emotions was a long process, but God has been with me every step of the way. He has never left me, and my relationship with him is very personal; I trust Him with my very life.

I want to encourage you, although it may seem as if you can't cry anymore -- as if the pain will never go away -- I want to share with you, Sister-friend, you are at the perfect place to have a real encounter with God.

It is when we come to the end of self, our strength, ideas, and plans, when he will step in and begin to fuel us with his power and love. God will meet you if you call out to him in that place of desperation. Open yourself to the process, take the journey. God will give you the strength to push past all obstacles, and you will overcome against all odds.

Igniting the Fire

The Outcome

I am now the CEO and founder of **Purifications** and the author and program developer of **"5 S's and a C. That's Me!"** Women's Development & Training Programs. I openly share my journey and give women hands-on application on how to break the strongholds. It is a journey back to the beautiful you…an introduction and journey to True Love.

The program teaches you the very essence of every area we as women need to become successful: how to nurture healthy emotions, the importance of becoming spiritually and physically fit, how to be financially savvy, and how to build healthy relationships with other women and your children…and it will prepare you to be a good thing for when your mate comes.

"5 S's and A C. That's Me" is my journey, and I have been blessed to share it with countless women for years. It is a circle of

Igniting the Fire

love, created out of my heart of love, and it is given to us from the creator of True Love.

Remember you are never alone… From My Heart 2 yours!

Pastor Michelle A Broadnax

Sacramento Ca

www.5sandacthatsme.org

INFIDELITY DIDN'T WIN
Elder Nicole Mason

Opening

I am grateful to God that our paths have crossed, and I pray that my story touches you deeply. Perhaps you have never experienced the hurt, anger, frustration and all of the other emotions attached to infidelity, but maybe you know someone who has been on the receiving end of such behavior. If so, please share my story with them and encourage them to purchase the book and read it for themselves.

Igniting the Fire

You see, when you see me and my husband today, you would never know all that has transpired in our marriage unless I take the time to share my story with you. We are extremely happy and madly in love with one another. In fact, that has always been the case. Now this may sound a bit confusing, but I promise you I am going to unpack this story for you, one piece at a time.

But first, let me tell you a little bit about myself. I am a mother of three sons. I am a powerful preacher of the Gospel of Jesus Christ. I am a prayer warrior, an author, an international talk show host, an attorney, and an executive coach.

Yes, I am a busy woman, and I am making an impact in the world. The support of my husband and my family allows me the time and space to do all that I do and to be all that I am. My husband is a great man, and I am so very thankful that he found me and now he finds favor with the Lord. (*See Proverbs 18:22*)

The Start

Igniting the Fire

My husband and I met during my freshman year at Howard University. He was a sophomore and a popular basketball player. We hit it off right away, and I absolutely loved his smile and his personality. I could tell why he was so popular. He is just a really nice person. He began walking me to class, carrying my books and being the perfect gentleman.

Now, I grew up an only child and a daddy's girl, so all of the attention directed towards me was just fine with me! And, it certainly helped him and our relationship when I invited him to my home, and my grandmother was just smitten with him.

This was indeed a first for this kind of behavior from my maternal grandmother. The few other guys I invited to the house didn't fare as well with her. She took one look at them and told me, "You can let him go, because he isn't about nothing!"

When my husband greeted her, my grandmother's response was very different. She immediately told me, "I like him, and he is a good guy."

Igniting the Fire

Well, I couldn't believe what I was hearing. Of course, being the charmer that he is, my husband couldn't get enough of my grandmother, and she started down a road where she couldn't get enough of him, either. It turns out that my husband was kindred spirits with my dad. My grandmother absolutely adored my father, and she saw similar characteristics in my husband when she met him.

The relationship was progressing well for almost two years, and then I found out I was pregnant. We welcomed a bouncing baby boy 9 months later. And then, shortly thereafter, all hell broke loose. I got a hint that there was someone else in his life. Needless to say, I was devastated!

It is important to note here that I wasn't in a relationship with God at that time in my life. So, my response was to do what he did – cheat! I know now that wasn't the correct response, but at the time, it felt right and it felt good to get back at him – or so I thought.

Igniting the Fire

The Struggle

This back and forth and vengeful behavior took on a life force of its own. I thought I had been in love before, but when I faced infidelity in the past, I quickly cut those young men out of my life! I couldn't do that with my husband because I realized that I really loved him, and I had another life to consider other than my own. I had to consider my son. The one thing that was a

constant in the relationship during this turmoil was our love for one another.

In the midst of all that was going on, the other young lady that my husband was dating got pregnant. He also had a baby with a woman he had a one night stand with. The young man that I was dating was murdered while we were together.

Time and space will not allow me to go into more details about these three life altering events, but please know that our lives were in shambles at that time. But the only way that I can describe our success is to say that God's hand was on our lives, and we were destined to be together.

The Process

Along the way, I gave my life to Jesus Christ, and my process of healing began. I realized that my husband was intimidated by my strong personality and my unshakeable will to do what I wanted to do in life. Now, let me pause here to say that those are good traits to have, but they can be detrimental in a relationship, especially when they are not in check and out of control.

I really didn't understand that early on in the relationship. I was going to have things my way, and I really didn't care about anyone else's feelings. If I wanted it or if I wanted to do it, I was going to do it. Wow!

When I look back on it now, I can see how we ended up where we did. Let me be very clear here – I don't take all of the blame for my husband's decision to cheat because he has explained to me

Igniting the Fire

that most men cheat because they can and they want to. He also explained to me that most men cheat because they are immature and want to have "their cake and eat it too."

I soon forgave him and forgave myself for my choices. I almost lost my life being vengeful towards him and being with someone else that I knew wasn't good for me. Almost losing my life was a major turning point for me. I learned how to really pray, and I started praying for my husband and our relationship.

The Outcome

We got married and began to work together to build our relationship. It takes two people to make a relationship work. It wasn't easy, and we had some additional setbacks along the way. But we began communicating with one another at a deeper level and respecting one another, and the marriage has flourished. A marriage can survive infidelity if the two people are willing to work together to make it work.

Igniting the Fire

There must be open and honest communication. And there must be forgiveness. God is able to heal our hearts and help us when we are open and honest with Him. My husband subsequently gave his heart to the Lord.

We have always loved each other, even during the crazy times. Our marriage was one made in heaven, before the foundations of the earth. It was love that covered our sins towards each other and towards God. (*See Proverbs 10:12*)

Many people who went to college with my husband and me are surprised when they see us, and we are still together. And we just look at them and look at each other and give all of the credit to a great God who knew what He was doing when He allowed our paths to cross some 26 years ago.

We have worked very hard and diligently to make our marriage work and to rise above our mistakes in the past. We are both very clear that we could not and we can't keep our love strong without God being in the midst of us. So, we worship together, pray

Igniting the Fire

together and talk about everything. There isn't a subject that is off limits.

We don't keep secrets from one another. We have access to each other's cell phones, emails and social media accounts. We understand that this marriage is a God send, and we want to do everything in our human capacity to honor each other and more importantly, we want to honor God. Marriage is holy and should be treated as such. Other people honor your marriage when you honor your marriage. You teach others how to treat your spouse by the way you treat your spouse.

If you are in this kind of situation, please know that you can do just like we did and win over infidelity if you and your spouse are willing to do the work. YOU CAN WIN OVER INFIDELITY!!

By Elder Nicole S. Mason, Esquire

www.nicolesmason.com

Igniting the Fire

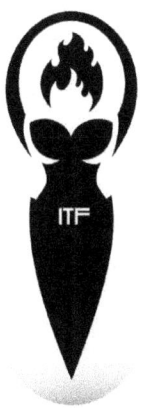

MY BROKEN ROAD TO DESTINY
Paula McDade

The Start

My story has written itself in my heart and mind a thousand times, but it's only now that I've found enough courage to write it down. Facing my trials and tribulations seemed overwhelming, but was very necessary, because when you see the ways in which God has carried you through the hard times in your life, healing, forgiveness, deliverance and gratitude can take place. Throughout

Igniting the Fire

my tumultuous journey, I can truly say that my appreciation of the Father has grown by leaps and bound.

As the oldest of four children, I was born to a young mother and an Airman father in the US Air Force. Their marriage was plagued by my mother's naivety and my father's demons that resulted from a childhood of rejection. After four years of marriage, my parents divorced and I never saw my father again. From that point my constant companions became abandonment, rejection, daddy hunger and fear, and because I was the oldest child, I felt the full weight of my mother's grief.

After my parent's divorce, my mother moved us back to Oklahoma and life as I knew it would change forever. In Oklahoma, my mother met a man in church and remarried. He was an usher and soon to be ordained minister. On the outside, we looked like the perfect Christian family. However, at the age of nine, my stepfather began to sexually molest me on a regular basis. I lived in fear, shame and dread almost every day. Keeping this deep, dark secret weighed heavily upon me. My mother had no

Igniting the Fire

idea this was taking place, and I would not reveal the ugly secret to her until I turned thirteen. Yet, despite revealing this secret to my mother, the abuse continued for three more years. As a result, I harbored intense anger toward my mother for what I felt was her failure to protect me.

The Struggle

As I blossomed into a teenager, I began to search for love and acceptance in the form of male attention. I became sexually promiscuous at the age of 16. I would have sex at school, in my house, in the boys' houses and wherever we could meet in private.

Eventually, I found temporary comfort in a next door neighbor and school mate who was a year younger than me. He was funny, a good listener and had a crush on me. I cried on his shoulder about girl stuff just like he was one of my girlfriends. One day after school, he came over to talk like we had done many times in the past. However, this time we had sex, and from that one encounter, I became pregnant with my first son Alex. I was only

Igniting the Fire

sixteen. After the baby was born, I dropped out of high school. In the fall, I decided to return to school, but did so under a great weight of embarrassment and feelings of being a failure. My grades were terrible and my attendance was poor. My self-esteem was below zero and I couldn't find anything about myself to love or even like. A couple of years later, I was pregnant again and one day prior to my senior class graduation, my son BreShaun was born. I was nineteen years old. Both of my sons were eventually sent away to live with their fathers. Many days I was filled with guilt over this decision, and this guilt would later drive me into some very dangerous behavior.

By the age of 20, I was the mother of three children, from three different fathers. Baby number three was a beautiful, bouncing baby girl. At this point in my life, my heart longed for something more permanent, so I began to look for a husband. I reconnected with a grade school classmate who I hadn't seen in years. We dated briefly, and then quickly decided we were ready for holy matrimony. However, our matrimony was anything but

Igniting the Fire

holy, despite having a church wedding, complete with dress, veil, bridesmaids and groomsmen.

I wish I could say that marriage settled me down, but it seemed to only create a larger problem. My new husband would soon discover the demons I had been wrestling with. Bitterness and rage had built up in me because of the sexual abuse in my childhood. In order to numb my pain, I would club hop and get drunk at least three nights out of the week, but I always made sure I was in church every Sunday.

The Process

As a young wife and mother, I found myself angry all the time. It would come out in fits of rage where I would throw things, curse, scratch and fight. I would use words like venom against my husband because my soul was so wounded. I was foul-mouthed and anything but submissive to my husband. Nonetheless, we always presented ourselves as the perfect Christian family to the

Igniting the Fire

outside world. This came easy to me, because I had lived this same dysfunctional life as a child. It was all too familiar.

Two years into our marriage, when I was 25, I ended up in the emergency room for what I thought was the flu. The doctor ran some routine blood tests. When he returned to the examination room, he gave me the news that I was pregnant. My daughter Jazmin was born that year. A few years after Jazmin's birth, I began to experience an ache for another child. This time I wanted a boy because I had not been able to raise my two older sons. I prayed to God and He answered that prayer when my third son David was born. After David's birth, post-partum depression almost threatened our lives because I was unable to care for him or myself properly during the early weeks of his life. My physical health also suffered severely and I developed a life-threatening heart condition.

During this same period, I began to desire a more genuine relationship with God. I had been prodigal for many years, and my church attendance didn't make up for the distance I felt from God.

Igniting the Fire

If it wasn't for my loving neighbors who were amazing prayer warriors, I probably wouldn't be alive today. They kept me and my family constantly lifted up in prayer, and even shared spiritual principles with me in a way that I hadn't been taught before. As I began to learn more and more about what was available to me as a Christian, I understood why I was being attacked so strongly. I received the baptism of the Holy Spirit with the evidence of speaking in tongues. Although I didn't fully understand, I had the feeling that my life would never be the same. I began to face some hard choices once I came into a more complete understanding of God's plan for my life.

Yet, even though the Lord was moving me into greater understanding of who He was and who I was in Him, I continued to face challenges. I found myself separated from my husband, as the marriage crumbled under the pressure of stress, illness and spiritual attack. While separated, I ran back into the arms of my first daughter's father and became pregnant again. I gave birth to another daughter, Devin, but the circumstances of her conception

Igniting the Fire

and birth were clouded with guilt because I was still married. I began to feel an intense level of anxiety and depression. After divorcing my husband, my heartache continued as my relationship with Devin's father also crumbled. In the wake of this break up and in the midst of a great deal of emotional shakiness, I found myself in yet another marriage with a man who was both an alcoholic and a drug addict. During the years of this destructive marriage, Devin and her older sister remained with their father while I lived in my mess.

The Breakthrough

Slowly - by Christ - and on the heels of so many missteps and unwise choices, I managed to realize the role that I had played in much of the destruction. Sorting through all the ugly details of my life took countless hours of counseling, many shed tears, and battles with frustration and anger. And yet, Jesus was with me through it all! By His great love, Jesus also provided so many

Igniting the Fire

divine encounters on my journey toward full healing and restoration - despite the choices I made along the way and the enemy's attempt, through these choices, to destroy my life. The many friends at my former job, church members, mentors and mental health professionals who walked alongside me were priceless gifts and blessings from the Father, and His gentle handling of me as I walked through the process of taking responsibility for my part in the madness has been life-changing. Through Him, I was able to separate my actions from the things that were not my own and regain my power.

In 2005, I was blessed to meet a man who was like a breath of fresh air. This time, I was able to enter the relationship without burdening him with the pressure to "fix" what was wrong inside of me. No longer did I see a man as a way to ease my suffering and emotional pain. Although there was still some healing to be accomplished, God was gracious. In June of 2006, I married my best friend, Charles McDade, and God has used our marriage to help me complete much of the internal healing that I so needed.

Igniting the Fire

Only an amazing God could use the very thing you abused like a drug, to turn around and bless you. Moreover, I can now love others with a different type of love while keeping my heart safe with God. He is my healer and my deliverer.

Today, I am flourishing in marriage, ministry and business because I am much more whole and free. I truly believe that the road to everyone's journey is intended to end up in the same place – at the feet of Jesus and the safety of His love.

Paula McDade

Website: www.paulamcdade.com

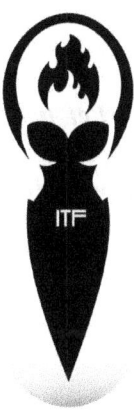

Don't Give Up
Rev. Areda K Stewart, M.A.C.M.L.

"Do not be deceived: God cannot be mocked. A man reaps what he sows. Whoever sows to please their flesh, from the flesh will reap destruction; whoever sows to please the Spirit, from the Spirit will reap eternal life. Let us not become weary in doing good, for at the proper time we will reap a harvest if we do not give up."

Galatians 6:7-9

Igniting the Fire

The Start

I want to take a minute to talk to anyone who is tired…anyone who is broken-hearted or simply broken. Maybe you feel forgotten about, cast aside, beaten down and abused. Or maybe you're just tired of smiling through it, tired of believing for it, (yes I said it!), and tired of hiding your tears. I want to talk to the ones who have been faking the funk for years and now are just too tired to fake it anymore…the ones who have tried everything in their power to be **enough** but still haven't quite made it there - so you're told. You have adapted and adjusted, changed and rearranged but you still don't seem to measure up.

I want to talk to those of you who are not yet delivered from other people's opinions but are constantly aware of who is watching you and how they are receiving you. You're the person who constantly bends over backwards for people, hoping that they will acknowledge you…hoping they will see your worth and validate your gifts.

Igniting the Fire

This word that I have to share is for you. So, if you are one of those people who just want somebody to accept you for who you are – unapologetically – please keep reading. Get cozy in your favorite spot on the couch or get your favorite snack as you snuggle into bed. A blessing is in store!

The Struggle

I'm a 37 year-old divorced mother, minister, and entrepreneur, who recently relocated to Georgia. Not knowing anyone or establishing employment before the move, I simply followed God and believed Him for the increase. In other words: I stepped out on faith.

It's a beautiful concept to step out on faith. You hear it all the time in church as one of the most important things a Christian can do. You hear wonderful testimonies of how God "made a way out of no way"… how He showed up "in the midnight hour".

Igniting the Fire

But it is only after you have trekked through the countryside of "no way" with temporary residency…only when you have survived through a dark and tumultuous 11 hours and 59 minutes of life, do you understand what those testimonies truly mean.

The Process

Walking out on faith is not for the faint of heart. In moving to Georgia, I've come to realize that I had to be *deconstructed* to be *reconstructed* into a stronger version of my God-purposed self.

This is the faith walk - the pruning process. On this journey, my sanity has been punctured and torn. My faith has been clipped and dead things have been stripped away. My relationship with God has been tested, and who I know Him to be has developed in ways that my pre-Georgia comfort level would have never allowed.

Igniting the Fire

Faith teaches you to stretch beyond comfort towards growth and the great unknown. But that process is painful. I have literally been balled up in my closet, door closed and lights off, hiding from my three children so they couldn't see or hear the fear and anguish as I cried out to God asking Him,

"What was I thinking?! Why did I leave everything I knew? What kind of mother removes her children from their support network? Did I make up that vision and plan??!"

I knew He had a plan but no matter how hard I declared and decreed, professed and confessed nothing was manifesting. I couldn't even find comfort in my first love, the church. And yet, despite all this anguish…despite all the chaos, I would still hear, in a small, quiet voice:

"Do not give up."

So, I kept holding on, even though I felt incredibly alone in my struggle. I knew no one in Georgia when I moved, which meant that I had no friends or family to sit down with or confide

Igniting the Fire

in…no one I could be vulnerable with and get encouragement from. As I mentioned above, I was unable to fill my emptiness through church, so instead I tried to fulfill the need with a romantic relationship, which failed in horrendous fashion.

Once again I went to my closet, broken and bleeding from my spirit, pleading with God to take away all the pain. I felt alone, rejected and now a failure on two fronts:

First, I couldn't provide for my family because, even though I had the experience, the education and the vision, I was unable to find a job.

Second, not being accepted or loved in this season of unrest was being translated in my mind by the enemy into **never being loved**. If there is one thing the enemy knows how to do it is to trick you into believing that you are worthless and less than enough. He knows exactly what to say to you to keep your mind in bondage to fear, disappointment, dread and doubt…to keep you so

Igniting the Fire

far from your calling, so distracted with the peripheral things of the world that you forget who you are and whose you are.

"Do not give up." I was lost and begging for God to speak to me. I would cry out to Him:

"Confirm I have made the right decision. I see others prospering and having testimonies. Am I not declaring? Am I not decreeing? Am I not praying and fasting and seeking your face? Am I not studying, tithing and seeking the Kingdom first? Don't You hear me speaking the Word over myself and others? Aren't I yet ministering Your Word? Where are you, God? Why have you left me? I know your Word says you will never leave me but why do I feel so alone in this place?"

I know I am not the only one who has had nights wondering where God is or what they must have done to deserve His silence. Not knowing how you are going to feed your family, afraid to spend money going to the doctor because you're not sure if you will need to save up for rent…contemplating packing your belongings

Igniting the Fire

because you're not sure if eviction is around the corner...wondering if you are going to have to expose your children to real life before their time.

Teaching your children to be battle ready and covering them in prayer because you know that if the enemy is after your sanity and faith, he's also on a mission to attack and overwhelm them, as well. Crying out to God in sacrificial praise while at the same time you're in gut-arresting torment, battling against yourself to know He hasn't left you though it sure feels like he has...

This is the faith walk.

It is not comfortable. It is not familiar. And it surely isn't just a good Christian thing to do. This faith walk is to develop the glory of God in and through you and it is necessary.

THIS is walking out on faith. This is the gory behind the glory no one talks about...not knowing where your provision is going to come from. This is truly knowing: **BUT GOD!**

Igniting the Fire

The Outcome

1 Peter makes it clear that the enemy roams around like a roaring lion trying to devour your dreams, your purpose, your God given goals and talents. He's looking for God's purpose in your life so he can steal, kill and destroy it. Do not get weary, do not give up. Your faith will carry you through. I share my gory with you not because it is over and done with. I struggled to deliver this message to you because the devil is busy.

But I will continue to sow no matter what because someone needs to hear TRUTH. Our God will not be mocked. His gifts, when we sow, will produce the harvest. It may seem hopeless at times, but keep sowing. It may seem arduous for no reason but keep sowing. Do NOT give up. God is careful to protect His Word so keep speaking over your life the Word of life and wisdom. Someone is waiting for your voice, your gifts, and your service.

Whatever vision God has given to you do not neglect it. Sow into your business plan, your educational goals, your family

Igniting the Fire

and yourself. God trusts you with His vision. **Endure.** If you sow into the Spirit, those spiritual gifts will produce a harvest in you. So keep sowing. Those who sow into the Spirit will reap their harvest. Stay focused. Don't give up. DON'T EVER GIVE UP. Keep sowing. Your harvest season is on its way!!

Rev. Areda K Stewart, M.A.C.M.L.

www.heresplanb.com

Temporary Resident of No Way

Permanent Citizenship with Heaven

"Don't ever give up!"

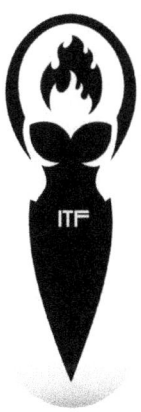

IT'S TIME TO TELL THE TRUTH TO SELF

Sandra Chaney

The Lie

Will the real Sandra Chaney please stand up? Will the real _____ (fill in your name here) please stand up? Do you remember the show "To Tell The Truth?"

In this show three people are introduced all claiming to be the actual person. Each person was asked his or her name. They all are giving the same name – pretending to be someone else. In this game, a group of panelists are given permission to ask questions of each challenger. The real person has sworn to give truthful answers and the imposters are allowed to lie. They pretend to be

Igniting the Fire

the actual character. Well "to tell the truth", I struggled with knowing who I was. I gave myself permission to lie about my past and pretend to be someone I was not. In other words I allowed other people's opinions, ideas, suggestions and thoughts to shape me. I looked for the real me, as the cliché states, in all the wrong places. When asked to really talk about me authentically, it was always difficult. I always started out with what I do, not who I am. This quest to find out who the real me was, all came to a head.

Fear kept me in a trapped place. Even though I was accomplished (had a great job, drove a nice car, owned my own home), I still was in hiding. Fear will have you:

1) Trying to please others

2) Over analyzing everything

3) Putting everyone and everything before you

4) Not fulfilling your true purpose. Fear had me thinking my life was not worth anything and that everyone would be better off without me. So I attempted suicide. You may not go to this

Igniting the Fire

extreme, however everyone's extreme is different. The truth of the matter is fear will have you living a lie. After a while the lie depletes your cup and now you are giving from an empty cup.

Acknowledging the truth

For a long time I was giving from an empty cup and did not even realize it. I pretended to be this strong, loving, corporate; had it all together woman; when all the while I was going home living a life of rejection, depression, loneliness and a heart full of secrets and shame. It was really easy to bury these negative things. What I did and you to, was put up a wall. I only allowed people to come but so far into my world. Can you relate?

This is where the acknowledgement comes in. Nothing will change until you can be truthful with yourself. I would see other women who had it all together and wanted to be them, but at the same time hating them and feeling intimated by them. Why? I did not know who I was and my cup was depleted. When you have not truly healed the wounds of your past, forgiven self and others

Igniting the Fire

you will continue to bleed into your destiny. I was bleeding and it was time for a change.

Attempting suicide was my cry for help. I did not know how to ask for help. It was easier to pretend. The suicide attempt forced me to start dealing with me. My cup was completely empty. God sent me several life lines; however my ego (the flesh) was louder than the voice of God. Looking at your own stuff it not always easy, but necessary to fulfilling your purpose and destiny. It means facing some pains, wounds and rejections that have been buried.

I dealt with abusive relationships, homelessness, single parenting, job loss, financial loss, and family hurt (mother and father). I had to stop and acknowledge my truths and stop the bleeding. The truth was, I allowed fear to keep me re-living my story. It was time to tell the truth so the true healing could begin. What truth do you need to face and acknowledge to stop your bleeding?

Igniting the Fire

A new life begins

Will the real Sandra Chaney stand up? Facing and acknowledging the truth was a process. Getting naked and facing self was a choice I decided to make. We have been given the power of choice. What will you choose? Getting naked is not easy; however it is necessary in discovering your wounds. New life begins where the pain first started. In your pain is where the healing begins.

For me facing the truth also meant facing the lie. The fact of the matter is those things I listed earlier happened to me; they are not me. Those things that happen came to teach me some things. It was up to me to learn the lesson. In the lesson, forgiveness was important. Forgiving me was paramount and part of my healing process. True forgiveness keeps no records and allows you to be truly free. A new life means you are starting a new chapter and moving on from the last chapter.

Igniting the Fire

I recently completed a 40 day surrender fast. I came face to face with how much "stuff" I had been carry and what it was doing to me. I was ready for my true authentic self to finally emerge. I was ready for a new life. In the past I kept asking God for a change from the inside out, but discovered I was not as ready as I thought. Remember how God delivered the people of Israel out of bondage, yet they kept running to and fro -- complaining.

There is a Sam Cooke song titled "A change Is Gonna Come. He states in the song "I was born in a little tent and just like the river I've been running ever since. I had to face the tents (shame, feeling unloved, not loving self, insecurities) that I was living in and rid myself of them. In facing myself, I went to my secret place with God. I sought him for true direction. In my secret place, I learned to start where the pain first began.

While it was not easy to truly see me, I was ready for a change. We are given the power and authority to rid ourselves of the junk, which no longer serves us. So it was up to me. I allowed myself to feel what I had been hiding. That was so painful and it

Igniting the Fire

hurt. I cried so much, but it was necessary in order to be free. I then forgave myself for self-sabotaging and playing the blame game. I also forgave the person, realizing that I may never hear an apology for them. It was okay, because I was choosing to love me, love unconditionally and live my best life. God's greatest commandment is to love. Even though, I hear it a million times (okay maybe not that many times), I finally learned it for myself.

Fear is the foundation of why we hold on to past hurts, pains, unforgiveness, etc. I had become comfortable in the skin that I was used to; I did not want really face me; and change was scary. I had been so use to performing a certain way. It was my normal and it made it really easy to hide.

What wound or belief are you holding on to that will cause you to perform, pretend or hide? It is time to release those wounds and/or beliefs that you are hiding behind. Give yourself permission to stop performing and pretending. Stand in your truth! It will not be easy, however it is a MUST! It was not easy for me. I came head to head

Igniting the Fire

with self. I was forced to really look into the souls of my eyes. I pushed past the wall of my wounds to see the hurt I was holding on too. That day I chose to allow the love of God to help me push past that wall. It was not easy; however it was so worth it.

Today is the day that you face your truth and allow love to truly expand in your life. Love is the foundation to all things internal and heals all things. I've been on a journey of self-love for a few years now. What I have learned is you have the power to create sacred spaces and moments where you can feel safe, loved and comfortable. In this space you can fully express your truth so that you can be completely set free from your hidden secrets and life challenges.

It was time "to tell the truth" and I am glad I did. A serious weight has been lifted and I feel very liberated. I challenge you to come face to face with who you are. Do you still have hurt, pain, unforgiveness, bitterness, shame, etc. in your heart? It's time to be free, so that you can fully be the expression of love you were created to be. You were created to be great! Your gifts, dreams and visions are waiting to be unleashed! It's time to stop living the lie! It's time "To Tell The Truth!

Sandra Chaney

Transformation Specialist, Speaker, Coach, Amazon Bestselling Author

Grant/Proposal Coach, Trainer, Writer Domestic Violence and Sexual Assault Expert

www.sandrachaney.com

http://twitter.com/smchaney

https://www.facebook.com/sandramizellchaney

Igniting the Fire

Igniting the Fire

I LEFT THE POSITION BUT NOT MY PURPOSE

Jeneen Jefferson

The Opening

I Left My Position but Not My Purpose is a portion of my life's story which in short illustrates my journey learning how leaving the position I held as a "Pastor's wife" had no effect on my life's purpose. It was the opinions of people caused me to second guess my true reason for being created. Their opinions made me feel that the only way I could be heard and effective was to remain on the platform of "First Lady."

Igniting the Fire

On the journey to my personal reformation, God showed Himself to me in ways that I could never express in words. I had always known that I was created to help hurting people but the ways were not quite revealed until I was forced to withstand my own hurt, ridicule, abandonment, rejections and slander by the very people I whom had sacrificed so much. It was during this time where God showed me that my calling was so enormous that it could never be contained within the confines of a single man made position. So follow me as I give you a snippet of my personal and spiritual evolution.

The Start

This part my story begins as most young ladies in the world. I was 25, I met a man; we decided to get married and begin to make a life together. The only difference with mine is that the man I was getting married to was a pastor. This requires an entirely different set of instructions.

Igniting the Fire

At the time my girls were 6 and 9 and my pastor and his wife were not in total agreement with the idea of me getting married to this particular person but they supported my decision. They would also tease me because I was adamant in that I did not want to marry a man with a title, including deacon, minister, pastor etc. Yet, I found myself doing the very thing I was so adamant about doing. I was living in Oakland, CA at the time and he was in Washington State. My journey was just beginning.

The Struggle

We spent approximately two years in Washington before moving to California. He eventually was appointed pastor of a great church in Fresno, CA where the ministry and lives began to bloom. Years after becoming established in the area, my husband at the time was ordained as a Bishop and had numerous churches and ministries under his leadership. I was the Women's director for our local church and district for the organization.

Igniting the Fire

In addition, I was working my gifts of speaking, teaching and ministering, throughout the state for various events. While things were great in that area of my life, I will be transparent enough to tell you that my home life was disastrous and a time bomb waiting to explode. It did just that.

If you were not in our immediate circle, you would have thought "this is a great power couple." That was a huge misconception that was portrayed. He was better at masking it than I was because I knew that God had a greater purpose for me than to put on a facade in public and be verbally, mentally and sometimes physically abused in private. I did not think I was being physically abused just because I was fighting back and not accepting it; I was calling it a fight..

I was teaching on domestic violence and needed the counseling for myself. How's that for irony. June 6, 2006 was the day that changed my life and a date that will forever be etched in my mind. t was the day I was not only separated from then husband but I was separated from my position as Bishop's wife

Igniting the Fire

and ministry leader and the only position that counted was that of being a mother.

Without revealing too much of the details and people directly affected by it; I will say that police, news channels and reporters were all involved. I felt like my world had all crashed around me. It was when I found out that people only loved me for the position I held and not because I was Jeneen.

My ex-husband was well cared for as the Bishop, whether he was right or wrong. But my children and I was treated like exiles with a deadly plague.

I believed up until that point that the people who called themselves followers of Jesus Christ would show the love that He would have shown.

We could not go to any church in the city because everyone knew me and the story and would become a spectacle. So I stopped going altogether. This is when God and I became reacquainted in a greater way.

Igniting the Fire

The Process

My process was a very long, lonely and lacking journey. When I lost so called friends, supporters, cars, house, reputation, finances I knew it was God's was of cutting back the people, places and things which would not serve my greater purpose in the seasons to come.

I was hurt beyond belief but I learned to accept and trust that He had me covered no matter how awful my reality looked. I was literally stripped from everything except my dignity and faith! God being the loving gracious father that He is did not leave me without a support system. It was a small group, it was all I needed at the time and they are still here cheering for me every step of the journey.

I knew that if I was going to recover that I needed a new environment. So in 2009, I packed up and moved back to the east coast to be with my family. It took me some time to really get my head and heart clear in order to regain my mental, emotional and spiritual health. Thing first thing I had to do was to release and

Igniting the Fire

forgive the people who hurt and abandoned me. I asked God why I had to be the one to let it go when it wasn't my fault.

He told me to look at both of my hands; one with the people who caused my pain and the other hand was ALL the promises and blessings He had for me. Then He said now YOU choose because you can't have both. Well it was a no brainer; I wasn't to let them hurt me twice.

Then I started reaching back out into the areas of my gifts and passions. I started a blog and begin writing again slowly but surely talking about my experiences and being transparent. I wrote a blog post called My Date with God at Wal-Mart and I get the most feedback and thanks from it my alone. In it I am transparent about being upset with God for allowing all these things to happen to me after I had done the things He told me to do.

I was beginning to be reformed. I learned that if I was going to be the writer, speaker and teacher that I was destined to become that I had to be relentless and forgiving! These two things are my

Igniting the Fire

life's message and I learned it through my grueling, yet advantageous process.

The Outcome

Here it is 2015 and I can say that I am undoubtedly grateful for every tear, sleepless night, lonely day and destitute moment. It has taught me lessons that I know I would not have learned otherwise. Currently, I am being placed in front of people who can see the gifts of God at work in me. My writing is also being featured in magazines and my first book called **Relentless Me,** is scheduled to be released this year. Not only am I a one of the speakers at **the Igniting the Fire Women's conference**, I am being invited to speak at other conferences as well as being a guest on various radio shows.

It doesn't stop there. All of this is happening because I knew that my position had absolutely nothing to do with my purpose. No matter what people said about me, I still have a future that is far greater than what I can think or imagine. So do you. If you have felt you have been hurt beyond recovery I am here to tell you that

Igniting the Fire

you have a purpose and a future that goes beyond any hurt. Your value does not decrease based on the opinions of another. Bruised yes, hurt yes, overlooked yes, misunderstood yes but it doesn't erase your value. I will leave you with my personal quote about my journey.

"After having endured great pain, I wanted to roll over and die but I couldn't. Because just like an annoying younger sibling, my purpose kept annoying me by following me around, my calling kept yelling loudly into my ears and my destiny kept tapping me on the shoulder demanding my undivided attention. #RelentlessME"

Contact Information: Jeneen Jefferson

www.facebook.com/RelentlessMe.JJefferson

Igniting the Fire

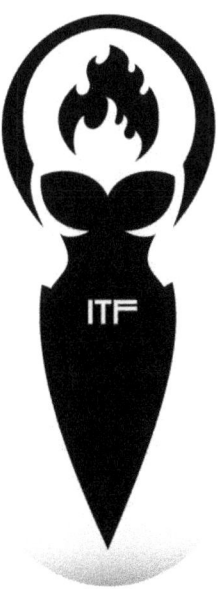

LaTracey Copeland Hughes

ABOUT THE AUTHOR:

LaTracey Copeland Hughes is a Fire Walker in her own rite- one who has been through the fire and continues to walk in faith while executing her life's purpose. As an Igniting Empowerment Speaker, business consultant and coach, Amazon best-selling author and publisher, she has bounced back to prove to herself that she can be knocked down but not out.

Igniting the Fire

As a survivor of cancer, she has risen from the ashes of what seemed to be defeat and destruction and emerged victorious and triumphant. Described as a gem in this season who has demonstrated that she's not easily broken, she has experienced success as CEO of the non-profit organization, Capstone Experience, Inc. She teaches others to do the same by thinking outside of the box and using experiences as stepping stones to destiny and purpose.

"I want to leave my mark as a professional, virtuous example; in my home as a wife and mother, and as a Business Consultant, Speaker, Publisher and Amazon Bestselling Author," she states.

Copeland Hughes is not only modeling the examples she holds dear, but also teaching the virtuous lessons through the Proverbs 31 Woman Project. Her daily life serves to inspire others and her engaging presentations help people to envision greater outcomes. As a speaker, she provides her audiences with the essential elements that fuel their own vision of entrepreneurship, leadership, purpose-motivation, innovation and bravery.

Igniting the Fire

LaTracey Copeland Hughes is available as a keynote speaker, preacher/teacher, workshop facilitator, in-house tailored speaker or for book signing events.

Email:LaTracey@LaTraceyCopeland.com

About Igniting the Fire: The Igniting The Fire Movement is about healing not just broken pocketbooks but broken souls! Together we can ignite the fire from within - through Passion, Purpose and Prosperity! www.IgnitingTheFire.co

www.ingramcontent.com/pod-product-compliance
Lightning Source LLC
Chambersburg PA
CBHW071453040426
42444CB00008B/1321